THE PROPHET'S BIBLE

THE PROPHET'S BIBLE

Gavin & Yvonne Frost

SAMUEL WEISER, INC.

York Beach, Maine

First published in 1991 by
Samuel Weiser, Inc.
Box 612
York Beach, Maine 03910

Library of Congress Cataloging in Publication Data

Frost, Gavin.
      The prophet's Bible / Gavin and Yvonne Frost.
      1. Fortune-telling.   2. Prophecies (Occultism)
I. Frost, Yvonne.   II. Title.
BF1861.F76 1991
133.3--dc20   90-41537
                                                    CIP

ISBN 0-87728-677-9
BJ

Cover painting entitled "The High Priest,"
©Karen Kuykendall, 1991. Used by kind permission
of the artist.

Typeset in 11 pt. Baskerville.
Printed in the United States of America

Table of Contents

List of Illustrations

Introduction

This book will show you how you can prophesy — and how to see your prophecies come true. Starting from age-old familiar prophecies that have incontrovertibly been fulfilled, we will show you how the prophets did their work; from this knowledge you will simply and easily advance into making your own prophecies. The ancient prophets were not skilled mathematicians or highly educated astrologers; they were simple, ordinary folk, striving just as we do today to make their way through a complex and sometimes frightening world.

In past centuries, many divinatory methods — cards, numbers, signs — have been given male or female attributes. For instance, the number 1 has always symbolized the male creator and destroyer. We have retained the traditional attributes in describing 1 in this book. That is to say not that we are chauvinistic, but that it is easier to comprehend the number by its old description. Nowadays we all recognize that a female in the role of creatrix and destroyer has as much validity as does a male in the same role.

Reading the old prophecies and seeing how right the prophets were, we are forced to the conclusion that time is a mystery and that there is a warp in time, a place where it lurches along rather than running smoothly. It will take you only a few moments with the aid of this book to see into that time warp and make the future a little easier for you and your friends.

You may have heard how complex it can be to prophesy using astrology or the tarot. In this book you will find no abstract mathematics; instead, simple, easily-learned systems will take you far beyond the place where the normal guide stops.

This book is intended as an introduction to many different types and methods of prediction. Using it, you can explore these paths and learn which methods work best for you. Since this book is not all-encompassing, you should then invest in books written specifically about your favorite method. Nor does this book contain descriptions of every possible method of prophesying. We want to help you learn to control your own life; we are not trying to provide an encyclopedia.

In the many systems of prophecy this book presents, we consider your interaction with those around you, not just your isolated future. If you hope to start a business, a new romance, or a life partnership, this book will provide the arcane methods you can use to prophesy the outcome of any turning you may take on the great Road of Life.

Chapter 1

A Sense of Prophecy

Five senses may seem enough — but you have more than that going for you. What about your sense of balance, of direction, and several others you can think of? Not to mention the sense of prophecy. The acknowledgement of your innate urge to prophesy is one of the few sensory pleasures the Bible does not condemn:

> In each of us the Spirit is manifested in one particular way, for some useful purpose. One man, through the Spirit, has the gift of wise speech, while another, by the power of the same Spirit, can put the deepest knowledge into words. Another, by the same Spirit, is granted faith; another, by the one Spirit, gifts of healing, and another miraculous powers; another has the gift of prophecy, and another ability to distinguish true spirits from false; yet another has the gift of ecstatic utterance of different kinds, and another the ability to interpret it. But all these gifts are the work of one and the same Spirit, distributing them separately to each individual at will.[1]

To justify our claim that prophecy is real, we could quote many well-known predictions, such as those related to

---

[1] *New English Bible:* I Corinthians 12:8–11 (New York: Oxford University Press, 1971).

the Kennedy assassination and the attempt on President
Reagan's life. It is more interesting, though, to examine
other questions — is prediction automatically self-fulfilling
(does the predictor or the subject make the prediction come
true?), or whether the future is cast in concrete and "written
on your brow" as the Muslims believe. The cast-in-concrete
idea is best viewed from the perspective of some of the older,
very long-range predictions. The startling accuracy of such
predictions, especially those of Nostradamus and of our
favorite, Mother Shipton, are well authenticated and are
worth looking at in detail.

Mother Shipton

Mother Shipton was the wife of a humble carpenter who
dwelt at Knaresborough in Yorkshire, England, in the late
1400's. She got into difficulty with the Church, especially
with Cardinal Wolsey, whose death she predicted. The great
Cardinal sent the Duke of Suffolk, Lord Percy, and Lord
Darey to question her. They got her story out of her and told
her that when the Cardinal came he would have her burned
as a witch. Hearing this, she threw her linen scarf into the
fire. "If this burn, so shall I!"[2] When the scarf was retrieved,
it was not even singed. Mother Shipton was not burned; she
lived to a ripe old age — while the great Cardinal died as she
had foretold.

Mother Shipton's rhyming prophecies are almost considered folk tales now.

> Carriages without horses shall go
> And accidents fill the world with woe.
> Around the earth thoughts shall fly,
> In the twinkling of an eye.
> Through deepest hills men shall ride
> And no horse or ass be by their side.

---

[2]Justine Glass, *They Foresaw the Future* (New York: Putnam, 1969). pp.
163–170.

Under water men shall walk
Shall ride and sleep and talk,
In the air men shall be seen
In white and black, and also green.

It is clear that almost five hundred years before they
happened, Mother Shipton saw the events of this century.
Giving her the benefit of a little imagination, are the men in
"white and black, and green" from the TV broadcast to earth
of the US-Russian space linkup.

And in those wondrous far-off days
The women shall adopt a craze
To dress like men and trousers wear,
And cut off all their locks of hair.
Then love shall die and marriage decrease
And nations wane as babes decrease.
The wives shall fondle cats and dogs
And men live much the same as hogs.

It is amazing that Mother Shipton seemed to have such
a clear idea of what the late 20th century would be like. In
common with literally hundreds of other prophets of doom,
such as the Hopi of the American Southwest, she foresaw the
end of our present world late in the 20th century, whatever
that means.

Nostradamus

We may take heart from Nostradamus: he does not see the
end of the world until the year 3797 on the Gregorian calendar. One of his quatrains notes that at this time paper money
will be so inflated as to become useless, and will be wiped
out. Perhaps we should pay careful attention to that one.
Like Mother Shipton, Nostradamus suffered at the hands of
the Church:

Dr. Michel Nostradamus

Sir:

You are hereby ordered to appear to explain your words to the bronzemaster before the Inquisitor at Toulouse. May God have mercy on your soul.

By order of the Bishop of Toulouse
at his palace. June, 1538[3]

Rather than risk the torture the Inquisition would surely inflict on a man already well known for his prophecies, a man whose Jewish ancestry had long marked him as one not of the "true faith," Nostradamus packed his mule and fled. Only in 1546, some eight years later, do we find him back in his native France fighting the dreaded plague at Aix. He cured thousands upon thousands with his famous rose pills, turning out to be such a good physician that the church no longer dared attack him. The old records are still intact; Nostradamus alone brought the pestilence under control through massive use of his new medicine. As the plague raged on he was called to other cities. Marseilles, Arles, Avignon, Lyon, all clamored for his services. Finally in 1548, loaded with honors and gifts, he settled in the small town of Salon, where his house still stands. Despite occasional peasant uprisings against him, he led a serene existence, and in that peaceful time he compiled his famous prophecies. They are arranged in four-line verses, called quatrains, in sets of 100, called centuries. Ten centuries in all are extant, some of which are not fully complete.

Because of church pressures, Nostradamus mixed the verses so that predictions for the distant future are mingled among those relevant to his own day. The most recent prediction to be fulfilled is the one that foretold events in Iran as the influence of the Ayatollah Khomeni grew:

[3]Edgar Leoni, *Nostradamus and His Prophecies* (New York: Bell Publishing, 1982). No page number.

Rain, famine, war in Persia not over,
The too great faith will betray the monarch,
Finished there begun in Gaul:
Secret sign for one to be moderate.[4]

The passions Khomeni incited while exiled in France (Gaul) caused a bloody revolt in Iran (Persia) that toppled the Shah. Then he came from France to Iran and caused unending misery — even before he condoned the taking of American hostages, an action that flouted all human decency and defied all ethical standards. It was a shock and an insult to all people — yet one man knew it would happen. Moreover, the man wrote his prediction *four hundred years* before it occurred.

Nostradamus, a patriotic Frenchman of Jewish descent, sat alone in his study in the late 1550's and saw his country being crushed and mauled by a mad German. He must have been horrified at his own visions. It is apparent from his prophecies that he studied the German aggression in great detail, for there are more quatrains on this subject than on any other. These are the quatrains whose accuracy prompted Frau Goebbels, and later her husband's entire propaganda ministry, to use them to exhort the German nation to unparalleled atrocities. The verses were studied in detail by a group headed by Ernst Krafft; through their scrutiny on one occasion, Krafft was able to warn Hitler of an assassination plot, and to get him and thirty Nazi leaders out of the building before a concealed bomb went off. A few of these prophecies make the point:

Beasts ferocious from hunger will swim across rivers:
The greater part of the region will be against the Hister,

---

[4]Ibid, p. 151.

The great one will cause it to be dragged in an iron
     cage,
When the German child will observe nothing.[5]

In naming Hitler (Hister) 400 years before his birth and
calling him a "child that observes no law," Nostradamus
performed an incredible feat of prediction. Hitler obviously
honored none of the universal laws of human decency; further, his troops crossed many rivers, not only the Rhine, to
come hungry into the breadbasket of France. The third line
of the quatrain describes the tanks and armored brigades
that led the German onslaught. How better could a man of
the 1500's describe a tank than "a cage of iron on a sled"?
Nostradamus saw not only this battlefield scene; he saw also
much of Hitler's life and death.

More than twenty of the predictions that Nostradamus
made from the hushed shadows of his medieval study are
clearly tied to World War II, constituting a veritable tour de
force for a prophet. A man who had no idea of tanks, of
airplanes, or of the man Hitler himself, described these
things as clearly as he was able; described incendiary bombs
dropping onto a city from the sky; described an alliance of
nations that were barely thought of in his day. Finally, he
described how Russia would attack through Austria and how
a handful of people would end up in that fateful bunker in
Berlin.

Almost half of Nostradamus' written prophecies have
come to pass and have been vindicated. Many predictions
are still in the future; they predict war and destruction and
disasters in the 1980's and '90's, but not the end of the
world.

Nostradamus specifically defines the exact technique he
used in receiving information about future events. He
placed a bowl of darkened water on a pyramid support;
then, entering a meditative state, he gazed into the surface
of the water and uttered his prophecies.

---

[5]Ibid, p. 169.

Being seated by night in secret study,
Alone resting on the brass stool:
A slight flame coming forth from the solitude,
That which is not believed in vain is made to
　　succeed.
With rod in hand set in the midst of Branchus,
With the water he wets both limb and foot:
Fearful, voice trembling through his sleeves:
Divine splendor. The divine seats himself near by.[6]

This describes unmistakably the work of a clairaudient as he employs a scrying aid. The technique can be used by any student, and we will provide complete instructions for gaining the meditative state necessary if prediction is to occur.

A Handful of Other Prophecies

Prophecy occurs not only in rhyme but also in such diverse things as drawings (especially comic strips), music, and sci-fi literature. There's a standing joke in Washington DC: you can always spot the FBI man because he's the one who keeps talking into his sleeve. It was in 1931 that Dick Tracy got his two-way wrist radio; and finally in the '80's reality has caught up with the prediction.

The most spectacular prophecies that have been fulfilled are those of Jules Verne's space adventures. How many more of Verne's ideas will come to pass? Will a giant submarine cruise the depths, commanded by a monomaniac? Will earth be invaded by aliens, if not from Mars, then from a galaxy far, far away? Even today we can see that these visions are likely to come true — yet when Verne wrote, they seemed too far-fetched to be anything but idle fantasy.

It is in Verne's writings we find a clue to the way prediction may work. He said that he mentally traveled to a "place"

---

[6]Ibid, p. 133.

where he could construct his entire story with all its characters and then watch them act out their destinies. He said he could travel to that place during and even after his writing effort and see his characters and inventions still performing their tasks and roles.

Making Predictions

From our work with astral travel, we know that spaces or places do indeed exist in the space-time continuum, and they are controllable by the mind of the astral traveler. If these spaces are actually in the future, is it feasible, credible, or possible that a powerful intellect can create objects and scenes which, when time rolls around, are still sufficiently intact to become part of present reality? Is the long-range predictor in fact sculpting the future instead of just watching it? In other words, is the future already written, as the Mohammedans say, and does the predictor view it on a stage and report back? Or is the prediction actually a self-fulfilling prophecy? Does the predictor think of a space ship and literally leave a space ship in future reality so when we get to that point in time the space ship becomes a concrete part of the present consensus reality? Did Nostradamus cause World War II? Did Mother Shipton in some way cause women to wear trousers? Or on the other hand, did they view future events as passive observers and only record them?

The predictions we will deal with are those made about the future of the "paycheck" world—the world in which we live. They can be about (a) the future of the environment, (b) economics, (c) public affairs, or (d) personal matters. As you look at this list of prediction-types, you can see that they start with those that use a great deal of historical data to make extrapolative predictions about the future, and end with those that have few or no historical data to draw on.

When the wooly-worm decides on the length it will grow its fur coat this season, it has combined information stored in its genes with immediate data input, and has used its prophesying sense to reach a conclusion about the temperatures of the coming winter. Its prophecy can be just as wildly off as can those of your weatherman. On the east coast the discrepancy between prediction and actuality is often more wildly at variance than on the west coast. Predictions of snow are often followed by a brilliant warm day. The weatherman has at his disposal more than 100 years' worth of tabulated data, together with vast computer resources; yet his prophecies are often wrong.

The famous German snowdrops that are never frostbitten succeed in predicting weather accurately only until they are moved from one locale to another. Those same snowdrops are often fooled if they get moved around in the United States. Their genes simply do not have data from their new environment. An apple tree which never gets frostbitten in Georgia will often get frostbitten in Arkansas or Missouri, simply because the patterns it learned in Georgia are not applicable to colder states.

When you turn to economic predictions, you can see the same mechanisms at work. Vast amounts of past data about the movement of the stock market are fed into computers and predictions are made. If you change the ground rules by introducing a new variable like Reaganomics or junk bonds, most of the past data become shaky if not quite useless; consequently the gnomes of Wall Street must search for gold in the dark. Their task becomes less an extrapolative prediction and more a process of successive approximations. This can be likened to the old guessing game, "Who pays for the drinks?" One person writes down a secret number and the others around the table guess numbers and are told whether their guess is high or low. The range of numbers narrows and finally one person guesses the number, and is allowed to drop out. Yet some of the Wall Street gnomes have more success than others do, so the word of one becomes law and the words of others are largely ignored.

In "Who buys the drinks?" there are three ways in which the number can be identified: psychic (you use a pendulum or some other device to learn the number); extrapolative (you consider all numbers the person has chosen in the past and extrapolate to the number he or she will most probably choose this time); and successive approximations (narrow the range until the number is eventually guessed). We believe the successful game winner and the Wall Street gnomes use the first two methods; that is, they use some extrapolation from history but (equally important) they also use a psychic ability, their prophesying sense, to arrive at their forecasts.

In the predictive category of public affairs, extrapolation plays less of a part and psychic ability begins to play a major role. Look at the predictions of the "Ten Famous Psychics" and you will see that some of the so-called psychics are just extrapolating from the Wall Street Journal; whereas others are using a genuine prophesying sense. It is interesting to note that the more famous the psychic, the less psychic seem to be the predictions. We have seen time and again that when psychics with good reputations have to perform on demand, they tend to fall back into the safety of extrapolative prediction and to shy away from the predictions their prophesying sense should be giving them.

Predictions you are most likely to be involved in are those of a personal nature. In most cases the subject will be quite unknown to you, and you will rely altogether on your prophesying sense. These predictions are often more accurate than when you are acquainted with your subject and extrapolate to a most-likely result from a knowledge of his or her past actions. The more you can get your mind dissociated from extrapolating the subject's past acts, and the more you can get into what we might call off-the-top-of-the-head or even off-the-wall psychic prediction, the more accurate will be your results. This is especially true if the subject is from your "family" in the sense that you are in some way emotionally involved in his or her life; because not only are you extrapolating from past performances, you are also analyzing what the effect will be on your life if the subject's prediction comes true.

In looking at four basic types of prediction ranging from weather forecasting to personal affairs, you can see that

TYPE OF PROPHECY

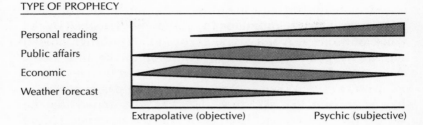

Figure 1. Extrapolation (objective) versus psychic (subjective) input.

the predictions range from pure extrapolation of past data through to the purely psychic prediction. Figure 1 is a graphic representation of the amount of extrapolative (objective) and psychic (subjective) input into these predictions. Notice, for instance, that for weather forecasting the main input is extrapolative with a small amount of psychic thrown in; and opposite "personal" you have a little extrapolative with the main information coming from your prophesying sense.

The Consciousness Connection

Every moment you live, your senses are inputting data to that fantastic computer we call a brain. Much of the input is below the level of your consciousness. We use the phrase "conscious mind" to indicate those thoughts and experiences that are immediately felt and seen and available. We use "unconscious" to discuss thoughts and ideas coming in from other planes. The unconscious may be equated to the Higher Self, the upper self, the ego, and all the other names given by various occult systems to those levels of awareness that are beyond the conscious level. It is not that we disagree with the attempts of various systems to subdivide and rename the levels of consciousness; it is simply that for our understanding of prediction it is not necessary.

Input into the unconscious levels can be of a psychic nature, or it can be mundane input that is overlooked by the conscious senses. A story typifies this: in a Washington hotel an elderly gentleman rode the elevator to the fifth floor. After completing his business, he summoned the elevator to go down again. When it arrived, the three passengers in it looked to him like skeletons. He was so stunned that he waved the elevator on. It crashed and the passengers were killed.

It is probable that this was not a future psychic insight; instead, when he rode up in the elevator he unconsciously detected that something was amiss, and that the awareness came through to his conscious mind in the vision of three skeletons in the elevator.

In considering how prediction works, you will want to consider the way in which the lower levels of the mind can communicate with the conscious level. Obviously interpretation of a picture or a shape vaguely seen while scrying, or even a series of numerological calculations in which you might unconsciously make errors, allow an almost direct communication. In the more mechanistic techniques, such as the pendulum or the casting of the I Ching with coins, it seems probable that the swing of the pendulum and the fall of the coins are affected by the power of the mind. Russian work has shown that weights up to $2\text{-}1/2$ pounds can be moved with mind power; and Dr. Rhine has demonstrated that the mind can influence the fall of dice. If mind power can affect physical objects and their movements, you must arrange your readings to let the minds of the subject and the reader have their full play.

Bringing the information you have gathered from the unconscious, and making it a part of your prophecy, is done by what we call the Consciousness Connection. You get data both psychically and mundanely; you filter the data; then you use them psychically (influencing the dice) or mundanely to give your prophecy. Figure 2 on page 13 gives you some idea of this process. You, the reader, are faced with a subject. You will use your developed psychic ability to help your client. The present-world data that you receive come in two forms: (1) the data that the subject gives you mundanely and directly, both verbally and in the subliminal body language that accompanies the verbal input. These data are always suspect; for only a rare subject will at first tell the whole story. (2) the telepathic data picked up by your psychic sense; often these data will not be confined to input directly from the subject; they may include input from psychic keys the subject has brought to the reading pertaining to other people involved. Such psychic keys can take many forms — photographs, clothing, and personal items from the other people who are involved in the problem will all give you telepathic links you can use to gain more information for your prophecy. Of course you cannot use this vast quantity of information if you are ceaselessly being barraged with information from the subject. You must have time for quietude in order to gather the psychic information and allow your mind to distill it. This interval of synthesizing is shown in figure 5 as a time of busy-work — the time when you roll the dice, cast the horoscope, or insist on silence while you scry.

Remember: if the reader's filter is biased, it will not accurately weigh the significance of various pieces of information coming through it. The reader must remain detached, calm, objective. The reader cannot, for instance, simply take a dislike to the subject — or for that matter fall in love with the subject. A superior reader scrupulously avoids

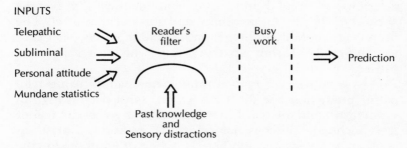

Figure 2. The reading process.

bias and favoritism, disregarding the fact that the subject needs a bath or ought to go on a diet or smokes heavily or manifests whatever unattractive idiosyncracies.

Requirements of a Prophesying System

There are three key elements in any effective system of pre-diction. 1) It must be a multi-path system; 2) It must include a reasonable amount of busy-work that the reader can do almost automatically while his or her mind flows free; 3) The subject must have confidence in the reader's ability to use the method of choice.

As an illustration, consider the act of driving across the United States over back roads. You will make many turns as you drive from the East Coast to the West. At every intersec-tion along the way you will pick a new destiny, both for yourself and for any passenger riding with you. At each intersection the passenger's opinion is solicited. The even-tual goal is clear; but many byways may have to be traveled before all the choices are made that will enable you to arrive at your destination.

A typical multi-path system is shown in figure 3 on page 15. At any intersection you can take any path. A route through the figure could resemble figure 4 on page 16. That path requires nine joint decisions on the part of reader and subject — and that's a very low number. Tapes of first read-ings reveal that there are an average of over seventy joint decisions. In second and subsequent readings the average abruptly drops to about twenty and stays at that level. The drop is attributable to the empathy generated between sub-ject and reader during the first sitting, which carries over to subsequent ones.

Now consider a typical multi-path reading using tele-pathic prediction and tarot cards. The tarot deck is high in symbolism, and any card can be slanted any way the reader feels inclined. Witches use one interpretation, Christians another, cabalists yet another. It is best, therefore, for the reader to know only the basic meanings and the paths so that as the reader uses his or her powers and the subject agrees or disagrees (either verbally or telepathically) interpretations can be modified to suit the direction in which the reader feels the subject ought to be guided. Celtic Witches use the Celtic method of tarot reading; this requires the initial selection of a card, the Significator, which most closely resembles the subject. This involves a choice among at least three cards, so the first decision is made and the reader begins to sense the direction in which the subject's thoughts are trending. A minimum of ten additional cards are used; in each case at least three interpretations are possible. It seems fantastic, but in a Celtic tarot reading there are a minimum of 265,729 paths. The reason for such a large number of paths is shown in figure 5 on page 17. Each set of three paths divides into three or more, so after the second choice there is a total of twelve paths (3 + 9). Thus the tarot affords a good example of a multi-choice, multi-path system.

When she uses a mechanistic method of reading, it is easy for the reader to try directly for a specific objective

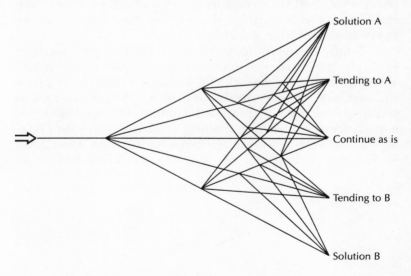

Solution A

Tending to A

Continue as is

Tending to B

Solution B

Figure 3. A typical multi-path system. For the sake of clarity, not all paths are shown.

answer. In a pendulum reading she might establish which team will win a specific bowl game. The results of a reading of this type turn out to be little better than pure chance. Flipping a coin gives a set of results just as good (assuming that psychokinesis plays no part). The reader must consciously turn this simplistic sample reading into a multi-path system. Will there be injuries? Will all the key players play? What will the effects of the weather be? These and any other questions that occur to the reader should be asked of the mechanistic system. This makes the system consciously multi-path. In contemplating each of these questions, the reader's mind is allowed to flow free, just as it would if a more complex astrological chart were constructed to gain the same answer. When a more subjective technique like scrying is used, specific questions must be asked of the scrying device, breaking the final prediction down into a series of small predictions.

When a subject is present, he or she must get involved in seeing the answers in the scrying device so the reader can observe those all-important signals that reveal what he or she really wants to learn from the reading and what he or she really hopes to achieve in life.

Totally unconscious methods, such as dream analysis when dreams have been directed by a specific question, are all multi-path even though the dreamer's choices are made unconsciously. For we direct our dreams. We are involved in scenarios that are under our own control. The symbology we experience is our own individual symbology, no one else's; and the guidance we receive is guidance from some level within our unconscious. If, in predictive methodology, we

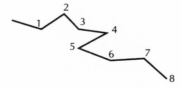

Figure 4.   Route through multi-path system.

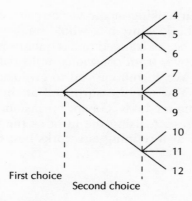

Figure 5. Path divisions.

astral travel into the future and view a scene, that scene is made of pre-formed assumptions that will crystallize in the future, for the future had not formed before we got there. At first it would seem that the ideal predictive method is to go into the future and view the stage; but we are not yet sure that the future is clearly written. In fact our evidence tends to support the hypothesis that when we travel into the future with firm ideas about it we sculpt the future to conform to those ideas. We have found that we cannot travel astrally to any time we choose in the future, but can view it only through certain specific future time anomalies — portholes in time. If this were not the case, it might be possible to follow a subject continuously into the future and see what happens at each of the decision intersections of life; but since we cannot do that, and can only view random future scenes, we cannot make a prediction from those views but can only attempt to confirm ideas.

We can take any prediction system and turn it into a system that makes it multi-path and includes busy-work. At some time during a reading the reader must dissociate from the subject so all those telepathic and verbal inputs are cut off and the reader's abilities can be used to synthesize the prediction. As we describe each method in this book, we will provide the steps necessary to get the most refined prediction we

can manage. When looking at the various section headings,
note that we will be looking at a whole range of predictive
methods that have been arranged in a sequence ranging from
objective to subjective, from conscious multi-path to unconscious multi-path. We encourage you to give each method a
good try in turn. You may be surprised at the results you
obtain by combining methods. Gavin, for instance, finds that
with the subject present, using the tarot as the main device
and the pendulum as a refining aid works best for him.

Summary

First: Prophecy works. So be careful when you discuss the
future! Second: Any good reading contains the following
elements:

> 1) Information gathering — Information can be
> gathered in a mundane way by direct knowledge
> or (psychically) from the various actors in the
> drama by telepathic and psychic links. It is this
> basic knowledge that enables the reader to predict
> from a good base.
> 2) The filtering and correcting base information,
> and the extension of base information by interpo-
> lation and by psychic means into the future. This
> is when the reader does the busy-work (or the med-
> itation) allowing the Consciousness Connection to
> work with minimum interference from the con-
> scious level of the mind.
> 3) Translation of information into a prediction
> acceptable to the subject. This could be called
> "softening the blow." It is not enough to tell a sub-
> ject that her marriage to Joe will be an utter catas-
> trophe and will end in a double suicide. It is better
> to suggest she do a little research with a couple of
> other guys before settling down. Yes, tell her you
> foresee a problem with marrying Joe; but many
> people are so obstinate that if you bluntly say,

"Don't do it," they will promptly do it! The whole point of prediction, after all, is to help people. If the subject flatly rejects your prediction and will obviously fight the result, you should try to reword the prediction until the subject can accept the result even if it is not exactly what he or she wants to hear.

Chapter 2

Pendulums and Dowsing

Dowsing for water and the use of a wedding-ring pendulum to reveal the gender of an unborn child are two of the best known and accepted divinatory methods in the world. Water wells and now oil wells are being drilled with the aid of the dowser's rod; and many gold prospectors swear by their doodlebug. The logical conclusion must be: it works. We are bound to ask, why? and how?

The pendulum and the dowsing rod as prediction tools allow us control over the instrument employed in the prediction process. These mechanistic devices for divining provide the dowser with an excellent means of keeping in close touch with what is going on. Many people argue that the motion of the pendulum is caused by joint psychokinesis (PK); that is, energy transmitted from the minds of subject and reader that combine to make the pendulum swing. If this supposition were valid, we should be able to hang the pendulum from a hook, sit around, watch it swing, and do a hands-off reading. Although some people can indeed make a pendulum swing under such conditions, it takes so much effort and concentration to produce the motion that no one (to our knowledge) is able to use this arrangement for predictive work; the mind is so locked into producing energy for the swing that the little half-felt messages of the unconscious cannot be picked up through the clamor. It is easier if we all assume at the beginning that unconscious movements in the small muscles of the hand or arm cause the pendulum to swing and the dowsing rod to tip.

Many people have theorized on how a dowser finds water. When he is out tramping across a field, it is realistic to assume that his unconscious mind picks up messages from the surroundings and transmits them through the autonomic nervous system so the messages result in spasmodic muscle movements which are outside the control of the conscious mind. Now, however, we must consider what happens when the dowser uses a map to find water, even a map which is covered by opaque paper so he cannot see the contours and the markings of habitations. Does the map in some way radiate information that the dowser can pick up? Or can the unconscious mind that once saw the map, seeing it now even covered with a piece of paper, instantly recall its most minute detail?

We have tried experiments using a map the dowser has never seen; the map is turned over before being covered; but often the dowser can select with great accuracy the spot on the map that answers the question. In searching for clues to a murder in Texas, we had three unskilled dowsers dowse a map none of them had seen, which additionally was covered and occasionally reversed. We marked their impressions with a pin pushed through the covering to cause a pinhole in the map. None of the pinholes could be seen by subsequent dowsers. In a map that was 20 × 30 on its outside edge, all three impressions were within 1/4 inch of one another. The map, therefore, must clearly take on some signature or vibration from that which it represents.

We have noted, too, that in such things as a picture of standing stones (particularly Men-an-Tol), even unskilled psychics can find points that feel warm and others that feel cold. This works especially well if the picture is placed in an orientation similar to that from which it was first taken.

For the rest of this discussion, to understand the operation of the devices we will use a modification of the definition worked out by the late Bill Finch, ex-President of the Dowsers' Association of America. Bill assumed that a connection exists between the conscious and the unconscious. (Remember that here unconscious means all possible levels of the human entity that are beyond conscious appreciation.) He called that link the "Intra-Consciousness." We simplify this to the "Consciousness Connection" or CC; for our purposes this is the link that enables divining to work.

Making and Using a Pendulum

Figure 6 shows a typical pendulum. An easy way to make one is to take a short piece of fine copper wire, form a loop at the top, and attach to the loop a length of fine chain about 3 inches long. Form a ball of plastic, clay, or wax around the wire, and you have a basic pendulum. Altogether it should weigh less than an ounce. It is best not to use magnetic materials or closed rings in constructing your pendulum. Try to avoid using such things as wedding rings and hair; these have personal significance and may bias readings.

There are many pendulums and other devices advertised that purport to do things better. Most of them work no better than the simple pendulum you make yourself.

Figure 7 on page 24 shows you how to hold your pendulum. Steady your dominant hand with your secondary hand, and let the chain drop over the index finger of your

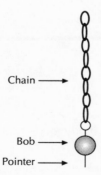

Chain ⟶

Bob ⟶
Pointer ⟶

Figure 6.   Elements of a good pendulum.

dominant hand as the dominant hand rests in a semi-fist but relaxed state. Most dowsers hold the pendulum in the right hand; but even some right-handed people are really left-handed by nature. If you don't seem to get good readings when you assume your right hand is dominant, try working as if your left hand is dominant.

In the system we teach to most of our students, when the pendulum swings in a circle it indicates "no." When it moves in a straight line, it indicates "yes." By holding the pendulum over the chart (see figure 8[1] on page 25), you can get indications of direction or of numbers. When the pendulum gives a yes or straight-line answer, the direction of the line over the chart will give directions or numbers. If the number is more than a single digit, ask for the first digit first, the second digit second, and so on.

There are many pendulum books on the market. We recommend you use one if you are particularly interested in pursuing this work.[2]

In actual use, hold the point or lower end of the pendulum steady over the cross on the base of the chart shown in Figure 8. Send a command from your mind to the pendu-

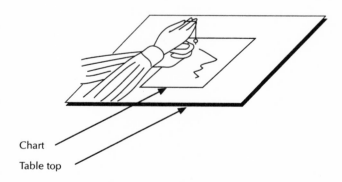

Chart

Table top

Figure 7.   Position of hands holding a pendulum.

---

[1]Such charts are available for sale, or you may make your own.
[2]Greg Neilsen and Joseph Polansky, *Pendulum Power* (Rochester, VT: Inner Traditions International, 1988).

lum, asking it to swing in straight lines to give the indication. If the line degenerates into an oval, hidden factors exist that cannot be simply assessed by the question as you have phrased it. You should ask questions similar to the original one but that approach the topic from different angles. Eventually you will find questions that enable the pendulum to swing in straight lines.

When the pendulum swings very erratically over the chart, your CC thinks you can get the answer more easily in another way; or someone is lying, and deception and unwelcome surprises are to be expected. When the pendulum swings in circles, no answer is possible at this time. The larger the circle, the more definite is the refusal. The pendulum should be asked then what the answer will be in the future. If it still responds with a "no," again another angle of approach must be sought to solve the deadlock between the CC and the question being asked.

In all, using the pendulum is extremely simple, satisfying, and effective. This is especially true when the reader can get the subject to run evaluations and get results that are similar to the reader's own results; for in this way the subject is controlling his or her own destiny.

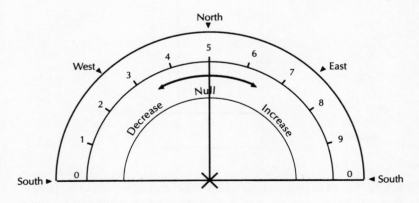

Figure 8.   Chart to be used with a pendulum.

How to Make and Use Dowsing Rods

Modern dowsing rods, constructed as shown in figure 10 (see page 31) are a great improvement over the old peach-tree fork. Holding one in each hand, tilt your hands so that the rods point downward before you, then tilt them back so that the rod remains pointing straight ahead of you but tends to be unstable.

Dowsing is one of the oldest and easiest of the predictive methods. The traditional application, divining for water, or

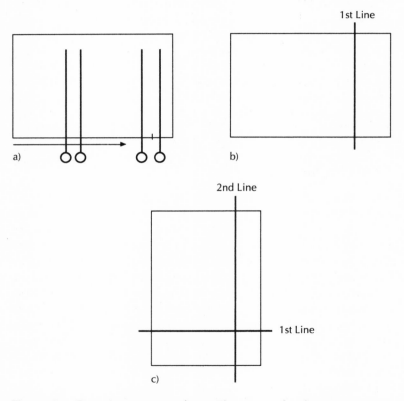

Figure 9. Dowsing over a chart. The example shows a person dowsing the reverse side of a map or chart to minimize personal influences.

water-witching, is only the tip of the dowsing iceberg. Dowsing for metal objects is a natural and easily learned extension of water dowsing. Using the angular indications of modern dowsing rods over a chart is just as easy as using a pendulum, provided you understand that the dowsing rod is an unstable device. When the rods are held over the chart with the baseline of the chart parallel to the shoulders of the reader (figure 9a), most of the time the rods will swing right or left. Let us say that the rods swing to the right. Move a little way to the right over the chart and dowse again. If the rods still swing rightward, move still further to the right. If they now swing left, move back leftward. Eventually you will come to a position where the rods swing in neither direction. Draw a line on the chart parallel to the rods from edge to edge, exactly under the middle of the rods (9b). Now rotate the chart through 90 degrees, flat on the table as if it were on a rotating lazy-susan. Repeat the movement of the rods rightward and leftward until they no longer move. In this way you will define another line (fig. 9c). At the intersection of the two lines is the target you seek. For best accuracy, a chart that is at least two feet along its baseline works best.

Go out into your front yard and dowse for the electrical and water pipes that lie under the surface. You will see that walking a straight line across the yard gives you an immediate indication of where the line of the pipe or cable is. From that point, make a circle; you will cross the pipe or the cable. Knowing that pipes and cables are most frequently laid in straight lines, you now have its location. Imagine now that you want to know its depth. Ask your CC to indicate depth by linear distance away from the pipe. Turn your back on the pipe and start walking slowly away. When your rods give the signal, you are exactly as far from the cable or pipe as its depth under the surface.

Holding a dowsing party can be great fun, especially if a significant reward (perhaps a bottle of good wine) is offered. Watching your friends work, you will see some start out by pure intuition and run extremely erratic paths over your garden; others will carefully quarter the area. A successful dowser stands at the property line and simply asks the rods to indicate the direction in which he should walk. As he turns to face the various directions available, his rods will suddenly respond. He walks in that direction and passes directly over the desired site. In this way you save a lot of time.

If you are asked to water-witch, remember to specify to your CC that you want good-tasting water at the minimum depth — on the owner's land, not outside the property line; and always try to find more than one site.

Asking the Right Question

The problem most of us face in using devices controlled by the CC is that they are the ultimate in logic machines. They answer literally, just like a computer. Basically, the mind is a very large computer with many sensitive interconnected electrical or neural circuits. Look at one of Bill Finch's examples: on a bright sunny day he asked the pendulum, "Is it raining outside?" The pendulum replied, "Yes." It will always answer "yes" because somewhere in the multi-verse it *is* raining! If the pendulum had been asked, "Is it raining within 100 yards?" it would have answered with appropriate "no." It may also go erratic or refuse to swing at all — because the CC apparently does not like to be called upon when an answer is more easily gained by looking out the window. The mind knows that using the CC will consume more energy than that which would be used by simply glancing up and letting the conscious mind get the answer. The questions you ask must therefore be (a) logical and (b) not as readily available through another technique.

"Is there gold in the mountains?" "Yes." The question is meaningless.

"Do you know the way to the Palace Hotel?" "Yes." The answer is meaningless.

"Did you walk to work, or did you bring your lunch?" "Uh . . ." Both question and answer are meaningless.

"Is Bobby still in the bathroom?" Erratic response. It's easier to go and look, or simply to yell, "Bobby, where the heck are you?"

"Can Midnight Auto Repair fix my car?" "Yes." This says nothing about the quality or cost of the workmanship, how long it will take, or how many frustrating interviews you may have to have with management and employees at Midnight before the car is satisfactorily repaired.

Be very careful of the way you ask questions. Do ask logical questions; don't play games, or ask questions that can be better answered by some other means.

Many people rely on getting exact numerical values from a pendulum or another dowsing instrument; however, in character analysis we find that except for that one well-known measure (IQ), these arbitrary numerical values are meaningful only to the operator or to the person who developed the system. We prefer to ask from the pendulum a reading that indicates tendencies and trends rather than specific figures. Of course the pendulum can be employed to learn specific numbers like the number of a house or the score in a ball game.

Using the Pendulum to Do a Character Analysis

Figure 8 on page 25 shows a very simply constructed chart. The lower dial can be used to learn tendencies toward either a lot of something or a little of it. You can see how a divining device could also indicate directions and numbers. Instead of using a very fine scale for numbers, it may be easier to break the number into its digits; for example, first ask for, shall we say, the thousands digit, next the hundreds digit, then the tens, the single digits, and even tenths and hundredths if such accuracy is required.

In character analysis we like to avoid the use of degrees, or positive and negative concepts. Look at the first entry in Table 1 (page 30), Self-reliance. In the center column, which we call Just Right, you see that the person is autonomous. In the Too Much section, you find that excessive autonomy

Table 1. Personal evaluation.

Attribute	Too Little	Just Right	Too Much	Reading
Self-reliance	Dependent	Autonomous	Brutal	_____
Honesty	Deceitful	Honest	Excessive	_____
Creativity	Passive	Creative	Destructive	_____
Appearance	Slovenly	Appropriate	Exquisite	_____
Personal relationships	Defensive	Warm	Intimate	_____
Group relationships	Shy	Effective	Aggressive	_____
IQ	Low	110	High	_____
Sincerity	Shallow	Sincere	Self-defeating	_____
Introspection	None	Occasional	Above others	_____
Temperament	Bovine	Stable	Volatile	_____
Initiative	Disciple complex	Suitable	Scattered	_____
Insight	None	Realistic	Unable to move	_____
Energy level	Limp	Achieving	Spastic	_____
Breadth of vision	Over-pessimistic	Realistic	Over-optimistic	_____
Dependability	Weak, unreliable	Dependable	Strong and reliable	_____
Initiative	Apathetic	Self-starting	No follow-through	_____
Attitude toward other gender	Hostile	Affectionate	Envious	_____
Sexuality	Indifferent	Healthy	Undisciplined lust	_____
Idealism	Expedient	Present	Quixotic	_____
Sense of proportion	Tangled in own underwear	Balanced	Overly analytical	_____
Money	Spendthrift	Sound	Miserly	_____
Domesticity	Traveler	Concerned	Over-dependent	_____
Loyalty	Friendless	Loyal	Parasite	_____
Courage	Coward	Courageous	Reckless	_____
Adaptability	Rigid	Flexible	Indecisive	_____
Sympathy	Cold	Sympathetic	Agape	_____
Forgiveness	Dogmatic authoritarianism	Appropriate	Over-tolerant	_____

results in brutality toward others. In the Too Little section, you see that an excess in this direction leads toward dependency. We recognize that our column headings may be somewhat arbitrary, subjective, or too narrow. However, using the table will help you get an excellent over-all evaluation of a personality. We leave it to your conscious intelligence to change the tables until you like them, and to your CC to make it work well for you.

When you do a character evaluation, you should record the name of the person, gender, age, and the date and time of the reading, together with the findings you gain in the actual reading. A quite adequate record will consist of little arrows pointing in the same direction as the pendulum originally swung. Typical records are shown in figure 11 on page 32.

When people come to you for a reading, the first thing you should do is determine whether they can use the divining device themselves. If their CC is good, they can; and they should, because they are more in touch with themselves than you, the reader, are with them. If you suspect, however, that all the readings are biased to one side or the other,

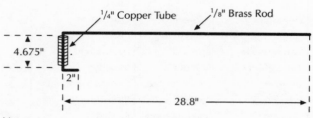

Notes

1. Make two rods, one to be held in each hand.

2. Make sure the brass rod can pivot within copper tube with complete freedom of movement.

3. ¹/₈" brass rod comes in 36" lengths from welding-supply houses.

Figure 10. Modern dowsing rod.

Attribute	Too Little	Just Right	Too Much	Reading
Self-reliance	Dependent	Autonomous	Brutal	↑
Honesty	Deceitful	Honest	Excessive	↗
Creativity	Passive	Creative	Destructive	↖
Appearance	Slovenly	Appropriate	Exquisite	↑
Personal relationships	Defensive	Warm	Intimate	↗
Group relationships	Shy	Effective	Aggressive	↗
IQ	Low	110	High	↗
Sincerity	Shallow	Sincere	Self-defeating	↑
Introspection	None	Occasional	Above others	↗
Temperament	Bovine	Stable	Volatile	↑
Initiative	Disciple complex	Suitable	Scattered	↑
Insight	None	Realistic	Unable to move	↑
Energy level	Limp	Achieving	Spastic	↑
Breadth of vision	Over-pessimistic	Realistic	Over-optimistic	↗
Dependability	Weak, unreliable	Dependable	Strong and reliable	↑
Initiative	Apathetic	Self-starting	No follow-through	↗
Attitude toward other gender	Hostile	Affectionate	Envious	↑
Sexuality	Indifferent	Healthy	Undisciplined lust	↑
Idealism	Expedient	Present	Quixotic	↗
Sense of proportion	Tangled in own underwear	Balanced	Overly analytical	↗
Money	Spendthrift	Sound	Miserly	↗
Domesticity	Traveler	Concerned	Over-dependent	↖
Loyalty	Friendless	Loyal	Parasite	↑
Courage	Coward	Courageous	Reckless	↗
Adaptability	Rigid	Flexible	Indecisive	↑
Sympathy	Cold	Sympathetic	Agape	↗
Forgiveness	Dogmatic authoritarianism	Appropriate	Over-tolerant	↗

Figure 11.   Sample of a completed analysis.

you should randomly check some of the readings and show them that they are biased.

When the correct question is held in the mind, the divining device will sometimes give you very surprising answers. The well-dressed neat-appearing person may get an excessive slovenly reading. Obviously this indicates that the person has dressed up to come and see you but his or her normal habit tends toward slovenliness.

All readings are done with questions being asked in the present. Thus it is possible for readings of such things as sexuality to be biased by recent sexual experiences or the lack of them. Similarly, if the person has recently been involved in some minor larceny, his "honesty" reading might not indicate his general level of honesty. It is important that you hold on to the idea of "current habit" instead of simply "this instant in time."

Before proceeding to the future, you must investigate all facets of all factors involved in the baseline present. This may include personal analysis of other players as well as analysis of places and things. If you are to do these evaluations, the subject must provide you with the psychic keys; that is, signatures of belongings or people involved, and photographs or maps of physical locations and structures. Only when all these factors have been analyzed can you start investigating the future.

Reading for Yourself

When you ask questions in your own behalf or when you are emotionally involved with the answers, we recommend you ask the questions "blind." In other words, make a list of the questions you propose to ask, number them, and have a disinterested person ask you for answers to each of the numbered questions. "On Question 3, yes or no?" Provided the questions are all different, this approach works; but in the case of reader-centered topics, asking the same question persistently in different ways is tantamount to playing tricks on your CC or on the dowsing device.

Further, when you divine for yourself with the aid of the chart, it is good to set up a mirror and view the swing of the pendulum and the chart itself in the mirror rather than directly. Serving here as the reflection of self, the mirror makes the conscious mind less aware of the reading, so the CC has better control of the divining device. If a subject of yours can use the divining device well, but fails miserably in divining his or her own problems, you should recommend using a mirror in this manner.

It is always sensible to break any problem down into its progressive component parts (this is especially true in reading for yourself) and in a forthright way to ask your CC to read on each of the components. When each component has been investigated, then the capstone question can be asked. Sometimes, as the answers to component questions emerge, the final question has to change because your path through life will have taken on a new direction.

Health

A separate specialty in readings is health, and Table 2 (page 35) suggests a preliminary outline of possible areas to be investigated.[3] Since most health problems relate to both personality and home circumstances, a health evaluation should be accompanied by a personal evaluation and an evaluation of the contributing background causes. Finding the health problem and guiding the subject to a successful cure by a physician will not solve future health problems unless the problems of personality and background are cured, or at least brought out into the open. Treating the effect is all very well — but treating the cause will bring greater long-term benefits.

Asking the pendulum to evaluate your own health is the trickiest of personal-evaluation readings, one that is nearly

---

[3]Readers can find a blank table at the end of the book to use for personal health evaluation.

Table 2. Health evaluation.

Body Part	Left Side	Right Side	Body Part	Score
			Reproductive system	_____
			Harmful behavior patterns	_____
Foot			Urinary tract	_____
Ankle			Digestive tract	_____
Leg			Brain	_____
Eye			Mouth	_____
Nose			Teeth	_____
Ear			Lymph system	_____
Hand			Nutrition	_____
Wrist			Rest	_____
Arm			Exercise	_____
Shoulder			Pelvis	_____
Kidney			Back	_____
Lung			Head	_____
			Heart	_____
			Liver	_____
			Stomach	_____
			Exposure to toxic substances	_____
Overall			Physical	_____
			Mental	_____

Name:_____

Street:_____

City:_____State:_____

Phone:_____

Age:_____Gender:_____

impossible to complete with accuracy. Be very careful, and use double-blind techniques when you attempt a health reading for yourself.

Composite Evaluations

A typical composite evaluation table is shown in Table 3. It can be used for such simple things as business partnerships or for evaluation of the future of a marriage. We believe the table is quite self-explanatory and you can very quickly let your CC do the work of running an evaluation. Do not limit

Table 3. Evaluation of a proposed joint venture.

Aspect	Too Little	Just Right	Too Much
Compatibility of leaders/owners/ partners	Disruptive	Harmonious	Apathetic
Will it fly?	Disastrous flop	Moderate	Blissful success
Materials/wealth result	Loss	Unchanged	Riches
Life expectancy	Early dissolution	5–10 years	Everlasting
Stability of location	Erratic, mobile	Moderately stable	Totally fixed
Offshoots	None	Some	Excessive
Regard of peers	Contempt	Neutral	Admiration
Legal problems	Constant litigation	Occasional litigation	None

your evaluation to the questions in the table if others spring to mind and seem appropriate.

• • •

Once you get accustomed to using a pendulum or a pair of dowsing rods, you can use your chosen divining device to help you in many things you do in daily life. The most obvious, but perhaps the most overlooked, is in selecting the best foods from grocery shelves. Which is the freshest lettuce? Which is the fullest-packed, best-tasting can of peaches? Such things can instantly be gauged. Finding those lost keys, deciding the best date and time to begin a journey, where to invest your savings, all can be rapidly and easily ascertained. Remember, though, not to take a single reading but to approach the question in little pieces. After each little piece is defined then it's time to ask the final question.

Chapter 3

Numerology

Some outstanding modern examples demonstrate the use of numerology to predict the future. The pianist Liberace received great help from a numerological analysis of his life that was done very early in his career. Originally, he admitted, he tossed it aside as the "musings of a maniac", but very soon he found how accurate it was. Late in 1982, when he became the target of a palimony suit brought by his chauffeur, he was not surprised; for this scandal had been predicted more than 40 years earlier in the numerologist's forecast.

Probably the most famous among recent users of numerology is Jeanne Dixon. She was rocketed to fame when she accurately predicted the assassination of President Kennedy in Dallas, and has since made many other accurate predictions through numerology.

The most famous numerologist of earlier times was undoubtedly Cagliostro. Such is the power of the press that his name still bears negative connotations, even though the man who defamed him was later executed and Cagliostro was cleared of all charges. His most famous predictions are still extant, being carefully preserved in the French National Archives. The three or four most famous were done to impress the Masons, for Cagliostro had set up a rival Egyptian Rite order. On May 10, 1775, before a skeptical audience, he correctly predicted:

Louis XVI will die on the scaffold in his 39th year.
Marie Antoinette will be beheaded.
Princess de Lambelle will be massacred in Paris by
four ruffians at the corner of Rue des Ballets and
Montmartre.
Napoleon Bonaparte from the island of Corsica
will be elected by the people to rule France. He
will end as a prisoner on a melancholy island.

Considering that at the time of the predictions the
French monarchy was firmly ensconced, this was a real tour
de force.

Cagliostro's most famous prediction was scratched on
the wall of his cell in the Bastille. A loose translation is:

Peace! People of France. On the 14th of July,
1789, this Bastille will be destroyed by you, and
grass will grow where it now stands.

As history records, the people besieged this famous
prison; it fell after a desperate fight on July 14, 1789. Grass
now covers the place where it once stood, as Cagliostro
predicted.[1]

The roots of numerology go back to earliest recorded
history. The Chaldeans and the Babylonians, who developed
the fundamentals of astronomy and astrology, also developed the basis for numerology. Many early religious systems
used numerology to prove that they were the one and only
true and right path; and through the Middle Ages the battle
between Christianity and Judaism was often waged with the
aid of numerological analysis done by learned Cabalists, of
everything from the names of God to phrases from the Old
Testament reduced through various letter values in both the
Arabic and the Hebrew alphabets. Some of the results of the
science of gematria, as it is called, were taken very seriously,
even though to the modern eye the way the result was

---

[1] For more information about Cagliostro, see Justine Glass's, *They Foresaw the Future* (New York: Putnam, 1969), p. 109–111.

attained looks farcical. Nonetheless, the science persists to this day.

In the late 1930's learned gematrians turned to numerology in Syria when they wondered whether or not Hitler would invade. The scholars were able to show that the name value of Syria was the same as that of Russia, and that Russia's numerological birthdate would ensure Hitler's invasion of Russia, not Syria. Needless to say, everyone was extremely happy—in Syria, that is—when the numerologists were proven correct.

The Basics

When the hidden numerological meaning of any word or name is sought, the first step is to reduce it to its basic numerological value. Table 4 shows values of all the letters of the modern (Roman) alphabet. This is the ancient Hebrew numerological system, which did not give a letter value to 9. The absence of 9 has traditionally been attributed to the fact that the old gematrians held 9 in such awe that they did not think a single letter could hold such meaning, for 9 was associated with the highest spheres of God. As shown in figure 12 (page 42) any name could be reduced. Notice how each number is added to the next one to come up with a total, then the numbers in the total are reduced by addition until the numbers are finally reduced to a single digit. The next step is to find the value of the consonants (which are

Table 4. Values assigned to letters.

1	2	3	4	5	6	7	8
A	B	C	D	E	U	O	F
I	K	G	M	H	V	Z	P
Q	R	L	T	N	W		
J		S			X		
Y							

Name								All Letters	Consonants	Vowels
J	A	N	E	D	O	E				
1	1	5	5	4	7	5	=	28	10	18
								10		
								1	1	9

Figure 12. Reduction of a name to its component numbers. For example, the consonants in Jane Doe are J, N, D; the numerical value is J = 1, N = 5, D = 4. When you add 1 + 5 + 4 you get 10 or 1.

regarded as the outer self) and the vowels (which are regarded as the inner self) for two more totals.

The Meaning of the Numbers

1 •

1 has always stood for the number of God, "The One." Since it is a single phallic-type structure, Christian numerologists always say it is male; however, there is really no basis for this. 1 stands symbolically for the sun with its power. In many cultures the sun is regarded as male, though in Norse and German lore it is female. It is best, we have found, to regard 1 as asexual.

1 is the basis of life and is the symbol of power and dominance. The 1 person tends toward independence, total self-assurance, and dictatorial attitudes which obliterate rivals; consequently 1 people become totally frustrated when they are in any subordinate position. They are fanatically ambitious and throw off all restraints; yet with all this, once they become leaders they are able to attract loyal followers. Their power is at its height on the 1, 10, 19, 28 of any month; and when these dates fall on their day, Sun-day, their powers peak. At such times they manage to become both intolerable and dynamically achieving. Fortunately by

the time Monday rolls around their powers are somewhat reduced, although Monday is usually still their best work day.

The two astrological symbols in which the 1 person works best are Leo and Aries. 1 people by definition (and by domination) automatically get along well with anyone who does not cross them. Their colors are those of the sun: the deep golds. Topaz and amber are their jewels. Some of the famous people who typify 1 are Alexander Dumas, William Hogarth, Captain Cook, Goethe, Edgar Allen Poe, Brigham Young, Thomas More, and no less than five presidents of the United States.

2 ●● Traditionally 2 has been associated with an artful, persuasive nature and has been looked upon as evil by those who could not resist its persuasive tongue. Because of its openness, it has been regarded as female and therefore evil (by those who feared they would be engulfed). Basically this is the fear of the person who cannot trust his or her own strength enough to yield to the passionate nature of 2. It is the number of the moon, which reflects the light of the sun so that even though the characteristics of 1 and 2 are opposite, still they are supportive of each other. 2 represents mental control and strength, whereas 1 indicates physical control and strength.

Many numerologists still regard 2 as a malicious and dangerous number. It has been connected with the god of the suppressed religion; that is, the devil, because the devil is traditionally regarded as the god of those not following the "one and only right and true path." Many choices given to human beings are assumed to be deliberately malicious because they are choices between two situations both of which imply loss. (You can't have your cake and eat it, too.) The most graphic example we can cite is from the Malleus

Maleficarum:[2] if a priest suspected an attractive young woman of being a Witch, he could claim that she aroused him sexually and therefore she was a Witch; or if he was older he could claim that she made him impotent and therefore she was a Witch.

The powers of a 2 person are at their height on the 2, 11, 20, and 29 days of any month. These days are particularly important when they occur on a Moon-day (Monday) in the sign of Cancer. 2 people get along best with number 1's, but they can also have meaningful relationships with 7's.

Some famous people who were 2's are Swedenborg, Thomas Edison, Thomas Hardy, and no less than six popes. The authors are still trying to reconcile this fact with 2's connotation of evil.

3 • • •   Numerologists rhapsodize poetically over number 3. It is associated with the best in us all. The Greek Trismegistus, "thrice blessed," used to be the formal form of address when one wanted to brown-nose a leader. 3 is called the perfect number because it has a beginning, a middle, and an end. It has been used to represent the male genitalia, and it is also considered to be the phallic 1 entering the female 2, thus representing creation. No superlatives seem enough for the numerologist when it comes to describing a 3. 3 comes through all the fairy tales and pops up in many aspects of life in such sayings as "third time lucky" and "3 handfuls of dirt to be thrown on the corpse," or "3 stabs to kill a werewolf," and in the multitude of tales involving 3 sisters or 3 sons, one of which is perfection itself.

3 people are creative. They rise to their highest levels when they are carrying out the orders of a 1 or 2—not the specific orders necessarily, but orders that have been crea-

---

[2]The Malleus Maleficarum, "Hammer of (Female) Evil-Doers," was written by two German Dominican friars, Sprenger and Kramer, and first printed in 1486. It was accepted as an authoritative work on the behavior of Witches and methods of torturing and interrogating them.

tively adapted to the circumstances. This is especially true in large organizations such as the civil service, one of the armed forces, or a multi-national corporation. They are trustworthy, and repay responsibility even though their creative urges sometimes get results that were not in the original orders. Their strong days are 3, 12, 21, and 30. They are particularly powerful during the times of Pisces and Sagittarius, and Thursday is their luckiest day. Mauve, violet, and purple are their colors, and their stone is amethyst. Mark Twain, Swift, Kipling, and Winston Churchill are among many notable 3's.

Whereas 3 has long been considered the superlative positive, 4 is the perpetual ominous negative; though currently it is losing some of its negativity and gaining a respected, solid place in numerology. It is a recurring natural number: 4 elements, 4 seasons, and many other 4's occur in nature. It was this very coupling of 4 with nature and the earth that made it "evil" to those who did not understand and could not go with the flow of nature but rather fought the Mother at every turn. 4's are rebels. They rebel against anything—ideas, authority, anything. You will often find them allied with a 1, a charismatic leader, who with 4's aid will form a new political party or movement. Because of their rebellion they are often considered quarrelsome; they make many enemies because they always argue the opposite side of a question—whether or not they believe in it themselves. It is more a matter of being the devil's advocate than any firm conviction—in a 4's mind, ideas exist only to be challenged. This is a person who has many secret enemies.

4's powers come to a peak on the 4, 13, 22, and 31 of any month. Saturday seems to be the best day, though Friday night and Monday morning are also auspicious. Because of their affinity for 1's, their prime month is Leo; but when a 1 is not around they tend to a 2, so their secondary sign is Cancer. For success they should wear gray; for notoriety, bright colors since they feel equally at home in each. Their best stone is a light sapphire. George Washington, Sarah Bernhardt, Lord Byron, George Eliot, Haydn, Huxley, Sir Arthur Conan Doyle share this number.

 5 is one of the oldest mystical numbers. So mystical is it that many books on numerology completely ignore it. It is the number that symbolizes the oldest religion. Versatility and bending to new circumstances typify 5 people. 5 is adventurous, breaking new ground, and shows a certain amount of sexuality. It is the male within the Mother 4. There is, however, less of the dominance of the lower numbers and more spirituality, more mental power than would be expected in an odd number. 5's are quick in thought and decision, and sometimes nervously impulsive. They should avoid all sorts of repetitive work. They are born gamblers and stock exchange speculators, always ready to run a risk. When they are down, they tend to rebound quickly. They never learn to take the slow, plodding route to success, for they live on their nerves and on excitement.

They can be very, very good or very, very bad. They make fine detectives — and excellent criminals. Their days are the 5, 14, and 23 of the month. Since they are obviously mercurial, their sign is Gemini. The best day of the week is Wednesday. One warning about 5's is: they cannot work with anyone who is the least bit stupid, for they are altogether unable to tolerate the slower-witted.

Mesmer, Handel, P. T. Barnum, and Benedict Arnold share the honor of this number with Shakespeare and Samuel Pepys. Light colors, especially those that shine, are natural for them; and diamond (in small stones) is their gem.

 The 6's are the romantic lovers. Their romanticism tends to mother love. Some numerologists believe it is the multiplicity of 2's that brings this about. 6's tend to be simple, straightforward people, and they like a settled home life. This tendency sometimes gains them the reputation of being obstinate and unyielding rather than simply placid and

domesticated. They love beautiful things; they make the most artistic home they can. They will fill the home with statuary, richly colored draperies and carpets. When roused, they will fight for their home and loved ones tenaciously and vigorously, even to the death.

They make life-long friends easily; their friendships last longer than those made by any other number-type. Because of their love of nice things, their sign is Taurus; because of their love of others, Venus is always important. The 6, 15, 24 of the month are their most important days, but because of their placidity, any day divisible by 3 is good for them. Tuesday is their best day of the week. Rich and royal colors suit them, and the emerald and turquoise seems to bring them luck. Joan of Arc, Sir Walter Scott, Henry Irving, Susan B. Anthony, Elizabeth Barrett Browning, Moliere, Rembrandt, Tennyson, and John Knox all share this number.

7 introduces the male aspect of domesticity: withdrawal back into the cave, the keeping of secrets and mysteries. It is almost as old and as mysterious as the 5. There is still an extant temple built in 2500 B.C.E. that had 7 gates; the record indicates that it was dedicated with 7 sacrifices of 7 oxen. The days of the week are 7 and throughout the Old Testament the number 7 occurs more than 50 times in various permutations. Each of the four phases of the moon lasts 7 days. Life's cycles are broken into 7's; for every 7 years significant changes occur in all human life. For this reason, 7 is sometimes considered a number of completeness; yet numerically it can never be a complete number. The 7's are independent, original thinkers. Underneath they have a restless nature, yet they are afraid to leave their caves. Consequently they devour books, especially travel and science fiction. Because of their wide knowledge, they make good writers.

7 tends not to care about material things, and can be touched very easily for a loan. 7 people often have very odd religious and spiritual ideas. They make things far more imaginative and mysterious than need be. They often have remark-

able visions. 7's days are the 7, 16, 25; all the days of the week are good for them. Because of their domesticity, their sign is Cancer. Dickens, Browning, Emerson, Bret Harte, Wordsworth, Rousseau, share this number with Carnegie and Sir Isaac Newton. Greens and yellows suit them best; moonstones and pearls are their jewels.

8 is one of the most difficult numbers to work with. It is viewed as two 4's. It has either all the positive attributes of 4, or all the negative attributes; there seems to be no happy medium. 8's are deep and intense people with much worldly involvement. They tend to be fanatics; they take up causes — which can be good or bad. They lack any ability to distinguish, and they never take up anything half-heartedly. They are fantastic successes or dismal failures. From earliest times 8 has been associated with a fatalistic approach to life. Many of the 8's you will read for will tell you that nothing they do makes any difference. The murderer Crippen was an 8; in fact in his life and his trial, 8's returned in combination with 4's time and time again. You need to encourage 8 to move from fatalistic 4 into spiritual 4; in other words, to move from a lower to a higher plane of understanding.

8 has always been represented by the figure of Divine Justice, and in Jewish mysticism 8 is one of the most significant numbers. Even today boys are circumcised on the 8th day after birth; and in some Jewish feasts 8 candles are kept burning for 8 days. A triple 8 (888) is the number of Jesus as opposed to 666, the Mark of the Beast. 8 is associated with Saturn, Saturday is its day, and when Saturday falls on the 8, 17, or 26 of the month, the 8 is in control. Their sign is Capricorn; their stone is amethyst. Dark tones and black are their colors.

John D. Rockefeller shares this number with J. Pierpont Morgan and George Bernard Shaw. But the losers are equally notable; Mary Queen of Scots and Mary I of England (Bloody Mary) also fall in this category.

9 is the number of the charismatic leader. Because it is the last and highest of the base (single-digit) numbers, it stands for great spiritual and mental capacity. 9's drawback is that they tend to be egotistical. In some ways they have a right, for they are resourceful, excellent in organization, affectionate, and sympathetic. When life comes off the spool for 9's, they tend to stand aside and let the disaster happen. If they fall ill, they will use every possible medicine and even surgery to cure the illness. An argument at home can very quickly lead to divorce; though it is often possible to get them back on track by pandering to their ego, and to get them to pick up the pieces of any catastrophe by telling them "only they could do it."

9's day of the week is Thursday; and when Thursday occurs on the 9, 18, or 27th, they are in control. Occasionally Tuesdays are good for them as well. Thor and Mars rule them.

All ancient mythology encouraged a fear of the number 9; perhaps because it was not included in early mathematical studies. Their sign is Scorpio. Their lucky stones are dark turquoise and bloodstone; they naturally wear dark blue and black. Five presidents of the United States and six recent European kings and queens are 9's.

 0 must be considered when digits add up to 10, 20, 30, and so on; for it modifies the meaning of the first number. If a subject comes to you for analysis of a name totaling 10, before reducing this to 1 it is well to consider what meaning the 0 reveals. It stands for "The All," the "Void," the ultimate spiritual force in the universe. So people with a 10 are religious leaders rather than political leaders. Their oneness has been modified and directed into a spiritual pattern. 0 has in it a great deal of love and friendship; it signifies people who will complete a task once started. Because of the Void connotation, it must be read warily; for if the subject has a lot of trouble, it may be that the Void is sapping his or her strength.

Higher Numbers

Certain higher numbers have numerological significance before they are reduced to a single digit. The first of these is 11, which represents higher planes of supernatural knowledge than any lower number. It takes the 0 of 10 and makes it a 1, showing that the religious love of 0 has been converted to a fanatical 1. Almost without exception, religious martyrs are 11's.

Another number that has had numerological significance since earliest times is 22. It is based on gematria of the Hebrew language. Because there are 22 letters in the Hebrew alphabet, and since Jehovah's word was revealed in Hebrew, the number 22 enshrines all the mysteries. The person who has 22 recurrent in his name is a know-it-all who can answer any question. Such a person is almost impossible to predict for, because he knows the answers before you give them.

Using Numerology

Figure 13 on page 51 shows our basic tool of numerology, the numericon. It is best made on a transparent sheet of plastic. For any reading that employs numerology you will want six or eight of these and a grease pencil. The first chart to construct is the natal numericon. The day of birth is used (note: not the year or the month, but the day alone), together with the birth name. Place a check (tick) on the numericon for each number that occurs. Jane Doe (see figure 12 on page 42) with birth date of April 10, 1954 had the numericon shown as in figure 14 on page 52. After tabulating her birth date and all letters of her name, her reader entered her name total five times. The number of times any number is entered is at the reader's discretion. In this case, a name of 10 and a birth date of 10 led the reader to make a subjective decision to increase the importance of the number by a factor of 5. Without this coincidence, the reader would have entered the numbers twice, once for the birth date and once for the name.

If your subject's problem is purely one of interaction with the material world, you will enter the sum of the consonants five times; if it is a purely moral or spiritual question, on the other hand, enter the sum of the vowels five times. You should decide the proportion of spiritual to mundane and enter the number of consonant/vowel ticks that you feel is appropriate.

Let us say it is a matter of love and marriage: What will be the outcome of a marriage to Harry Woods on December 5th? You will need to make a numericon for Harry Woods and another for Jane Woods, including in the latter the key natal date of the wedding. See figure 15 on page 53. Conso-

Name: _____

Numbers: _____

Consonants: _____ Vowels: _____

Birth date: _____

1									
2									
3									
4									
5									
6									
7									
8									
9									
0									
11									
22									

Figure 13. The numericon.

nants are considered to reflect the material world; vowels are considered to reflect the spiritual world. In a marriage, one looks for more spiritual content than material. The reader makes the decision as to the number of times they multiply the consonants and vowels. Typically, in a marriage situation you use twice the consonants and twice the vowels.

A comparison of the numericons shows that marriage could be balanced: the change of names will make Jane less dominant and perhaps less religious. The preponderance of 5 leads to some concern. Although the couple will stay in the Old Religion, their marriage will be very adventuresome and have many highs and lows as they impulsively change jobs and move around the country.

Name: __Jane   Doe_____

Numbers: __1155   475   =   28   =   10 = 1__

Consonants: ___10 = 1_____ Vowels: ___18 = 9___

Birth date: __April 10, 1954 = 10_____

1	X	X	X	X	X	X			
2									
3									
4									
5									
6									
7									
8									
9									
0	X	X	X	X	X	X			
11									
22									

Figure 14.   Jane Doe's natal numericon.

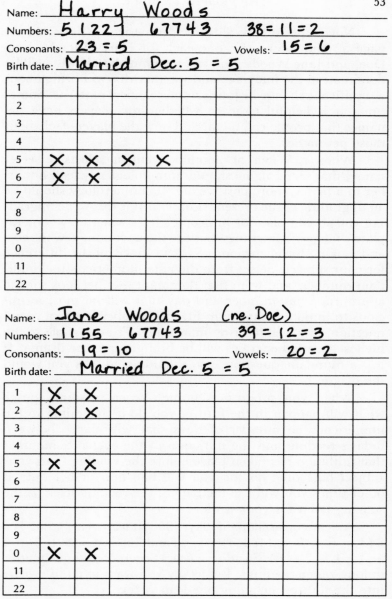

Name: __Harry Woods__

Numbers: __5 1 2 2 7   6 7 7 4 3   38 = 11 = 2__

Consonants: __23 = 5__   Vowels: __15 = 6__

Birth date: __Married   Dec. 5 = 5__

1											
2											
3											
4											
5	X	X	X	X							
6	X	X									
7											
8											
9											
0											
11											
22											

Name: __Jane   Woods   (ne. Doe)__

Numbers: __1 1 5 5   6 7 7 4 3   39 = 12 = 3__

Consonants: __19 = 10__   Vowels: __20 = 2__

Birth date: __Married   Dec. 5 = 5__

1	X	X									
2	X	X									
3											
4											
5	X	X									
6											
7											
8											
9											
0	X	X									
11											
22											

Figure 15.   Analyzing a marriage.

Now superimpose all three Numericons (figure 14 on page 52 and figure 15): one each for Harry Woods, Jane Doe, and Jane Woods. You can see immediately who will be dominant in the marriage and whether this will bring about a significant change in Jane's numerological patterns. Sometimes it is helpful to learn whether the players have pet names that people call them, and how the players feel about those pet names.

When a Witch or another occultist selects a secret name, that secret name should numerologically lead him or her to a better, more positive life. Its numerology should be an upgrading of the present situation. It is this same upgrading you should plan for in people's lives when they contemplate changes. Sometimes plotting the upcoming few months and looking for auspicious days can make all the difference for your subject. Select from the natal numericon the dominant number; and from that dominant number look for the appropriate day-number and day that will be most auspicious to initiate a change in life. Remember if it is a moral question, it is well to bring in as many 0's as possible so the highest spiritual energies will be brought into the drama. If it is a mundane question, you should avoid 0 as you would the plague.

When you progress a numerological reading to see what will happen in the future, you do it by adding to the numericon the number of days that will elapse between today's reading and the initiation of the event. Sometimes that initiation has taken place before the reading, and your subject has come hoping you will bail him or her out; at other times you will use the date of the reading itself as the starting point for your work.

A year consists of 365 days (366 in leap years). 365 is a 5 (3 + 6 + 5 = 14; 1 + 4 = 5) and 366 is a 6 (3 + 6 + 6 = 15; 1 + 5 = 6). So adding years becomes a simple matter in long-range readings. Let us say you want to go five years into the future (including one leap year):

4 ordinary years (each count 5) 4 × 5 = 20
+ 1 leap year (each count 6)   1 × 6 = 6
                                20 + 6 = 26 = 2 + 6 = 8

Add another 8, then, to all the numericons of the case.

Summary

Numerology is one of the oldest predictive methods and one that is easy to understand and to use. It allows full play of the psychic senses while the busy-work of completing the numericons is accomplished. Selection of the dominant numbers from the numericons must always consider the secondary numbers that serve as the modifiers of the situation. Thus a numericon reading is not as cut and dried or as mechanistic as might at first glance be supposed. Instead, it is a very powerful and subtle system.

Chapter 4

Domino Divination

The game of dominoes is played extensively in the pubs and beerhalls of northern Europe. Use of the tiles[1] as a divining aid is almost unknown outside those gathering places, yet the tiles constitute a very powerful and most easily learned method of prophecy. The same problems beset the pub-goers as beset us all, and prediction is just as important to them as it is to us. With their earthy background, it is not surprising that interpretations tend to be rather coarse. We have retained some of the forthrightness, but polished the meanings here and there to make them more acceptable to a sophisticated readership.

The ancient Chinese game of Mah Jongg uses tiles as dominoes does. Mah Jongg tiles have been used for centuries to divine in China. Domino divination is a very powerful method, the use of which was first brought into print by Sybil Leek. Since that time it has grown rapidly in favor as being a western divinatory method that is at least as effective as Mah Jongg or the *I Ching*. The readily available dominoes method deserves to be more widely used.

---

[1]Wooden Double-Six domino set. Twenty-eight wooden tiles, available at most toy stores.

Reading the Tiles

Reading dominoes seems deceptively easy, but it is vital that you avoid the natural tendency to read quickly. Instead dwell on the tiles. The longer you consider them, the more your Consciousness Connection helps you get the right meanings.

In a reading, the subject lays the tiles face down on a slippery surface. He or she scrambles them thoroughly and draws three tiles from the set, placing them face upward before the reader as shown in figure 16. The tile to the left (closest to the reader) indicates the basis for the question. The second tile shows the present; the tile uppermost and to the right (closest to the subject) tells the future.

The tiles are read first for their basic meanings as given in the next section. Crossings are a point of contact where two tiles butt up to each other. They are the transitional points in any reading.

Meanings of the Crossings

- The same number in both spaces denotes a smooth transition, one in which no changes are seen in life or in circumstances.
- A transition whose left-hand number is lower than its right-hand number denotes an improvement in circumstances.

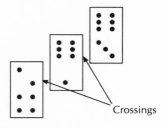

Figure 16.   A domino reading.

- A crossing whose left-hand number is larger than its right-hand number denotes misfortune. The scale of the misfortune is gauged by the difference (the point spread) in the numbers; the larger the point spread, the greater will be the misfortune.
- If the right-hand number is blank, this is the ultimate misfortune; for nothing that can be done will overcome the Void. It means that death of the old enterprise will take place and an entirely new beginning will be undertaken.

Careful review of the crossings can often show the best course of action or what will be the solution of a problem at a crossing. Understanding is gained by averaging the crossing numbers. (Add the two numbers together and divide the sum by 2.) Refer to the text for the meaning of the crossing.

Meanings of the Numbers

The 28 wooden tiles that constitute the set of dominoes used for divination range from double blank to double 6. So you may understand them more easily, each number is assigned a meaning. The reader considers the interplay between the numbers to learn the interpretation of each tile. Since each tile (except the doubles) can be positioned upright or reversed, 49 specific meanings are available. If you remember the basic meaning and symbology of each number, you can readily infer the meaning of the tile, or let your Consciousness Connection give you the significance of the tile as it pertains to this specific reading. Many of the dies have specific male or female energies. Just as in other systems of divination (such as tarot cards), when a male-energy turns up in a female reading, we are considering the type of energy, not the gender of the subject. If an all-mother (6) turns up where we are considering a father, the person or question under consideration has motherly, nurturing

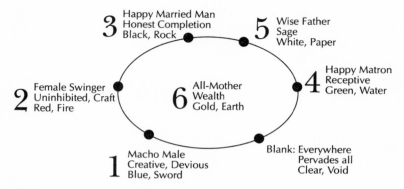

Figure 17.   Domino number attributes.

attributes. This is not a sexist or chauvinistic interpretation of the dice; it is just the way their energies are visualized.

As in many systems of prophecy, thinking of the numbers as human types can be a great aid to understanding, as shown in figure 17. You may want to extend this idea and use, for instance, characters from TV shows as your archetypes. The interaction between a Fonzie and a Sheriff Lobo can readily be imagined. If visualization of this sort helps you, by all means use it.

The blank denotes the Void, and Nothing. Often in a reading it means, "Nothing will come of it. Something only prayer can help." It pervades everything. It is not thought of as above but rather as everywhere. Energy put into it is totally lost, for it represents a vacuum that will suck up anything. Blank has no visible color, yet it is all colors. It has one special attribute: in the context of the reading it can mean gaining spiritual awareness or going into the priesthood, becoming a "black beetle," as the pub-goer would say.

1 • This is the man in the prime of his life. He is perennially horny; he always has an erection inside his blue jeans. He is continually trying to impregnate the female, constantly trying to create. Any time he is unleashed, he will lay everything in sight. He is represented by the Sword in its creating-through-destroying aspect. He takes the color blue of the worker; he is deceitful when it furthers his aims. The town's irresponsible macho male. Anything new and different has to become a notch on his headboard. In Europe he is the spiv or the flic; in America perhaps the most horny of the motorcycle gang.

2 The female principle in its most basic sexual attitude. She is eager to be impregnated. She does not count the cost. The nicest way of saying it is, "She's the town's known redheaded swinger, going for a quick lay." She is the adventurous female, a fighting, scratching cat; she is creative and a craftswoman[2] or a military nurse. She gets the color red and the attributes of fire.

3 The married man. There is more stability here. He lies content between his wife's legs. He is still creative, but now he has more responsibility and is anchored firmly to one woman. He is the young head of a family, as firm as a rock. When he is a bright type, he can be considered a rock/jewel. He wears the black or dark gray suit of business and may be henpecked.

4 The housewife coming into her own. She has had children and is content. She understands her feminine role and its powers. It is a tile of stillness and repose, yet one of abundance. It typifies the healthy, vibrant young matron. She is like water, flowing into her surroundings. Things

---

[2]"Craft" in this context means handcraft, career or job.

thrown into her may color her behavior — but often they sink out of sight, absorbed in her placidity. Because of her intuition and her child-bearing potential, she is thought of as new beginnings and the green growth of spring.

 The old man. The esteem and repose of the woman are being given to the old man. He is surrounded by available femininity, but can use none of it. He is old and "off it," yet with the stilling of his creative urges come wisdom and insight. He sits above and back from the world. His hair is white; he thinks of himself as a sage. He dreams, and writes his dreams. When written down, his ideas bear some weight. He can withstand onslaughts from the Sword of 1 or the Fire of 2, but he is attracted by the fire and sometimes even burned. He can easily control 3; for as the Chinese say, "Paper wraps rock."

 The elderly lady, the wise woman. She is beyond the need for a male partner; yet the two 3's here reveal that she has had her share of the joy of life. She represents good fortune, wealth, and happiness. This is probably because in earlier times men tended to die young, and healthy women became leaders of group, family, and clan because they had more knowledge of the world and wisdom available than did anyone else. Her wealth is rooted in the soil, and in the soil she finds gold. She can also represent Mother Nature.

An easy way to memorize these seven sets of attributes is as shown in the three-dimensional representation shown in figure 17 (page 60). You can expand on the attributes in any way you like: make them living people, perhaps like some of your acquaintances.

Tile Meanings

Blank-Blank — This is the first of the doubling tiles. It piles misfortune on misfortune. Nothing can pass it. When it turns up in the future, a way around it must be found, a new path followed. It is positive only when someone is thinking of going into religious fields or when someone is about to die of a painful disease; in the latter case it signifies death and release. In all other enterprises the blank-blank is nothing but trouble.

Meaning: Stop putting money and effort into something that's going nowhere. Find a new path. Become a priest. Only prayer can help.

1–1: Here you have the macho male doubling. It represents fabulous creativity, but the creativity can often be accompanied by destruction. In an enterprise the old enterprise will break down; but from this will arise a new, more powerful business in the future. The tile can also represent lies, as well as someone whose brains are draining out through their genitalia because of too much lustful activity.

Meaning: Think about your obsessive urge to do something. Make sure that in the end it is really creative. Sudden unexpected changes.

2–2: This tile might well apply to the town whore — yet it also applies to the dedicated craftsperson who will let nothing stand in the way. One can imagine a pop singer who sings extravagantly and differently and who has broken down barriers to the career by use of his or her sexuality. This person is fiery and will not be crossed. The tile shows short-term dedication and determination — the highest and most intense female tigress-like commitment, especially to her litter.

Meaning: Beware of the motives of someone who too blatantly wants to bed you. On a different level: beware the backer who too readily gives you money. The end may justify the means.

3–3: The positive aspects of the happily married person are doubled here. The tireless, honest, steadfast person who works forever toward that small promotion, toward keeping the family together, who goes to the boring job every day. This person is boring, but he or she is also the rock supporting family life and much of the nation's industry.

Meaning: Success and good fortune through hard work. It may take longer than expected, but success is assured and solid.

4–4: On the surface this is the doubling of the happy, mature, stable person; but there is some conflict here, some unresolved emotions. This tile is the ultimate in receptivity; it is symbolized by the all-enveloping water. Beware, for it envelops so entirely that it has tendencies resembling those of the Void. It can drown you in "love." It has also the persistent energy of moving water that can eventually wear away any obstacle. Where intuition and subjectivity are important, this is the best tile. Following its intuition leads to great success.

Meaning: Hidden problems. Great persistence brings great success. Drifting with the tide is unlucky.

5–5: This double also has some conflict within it. Two sages have different views about the correct course to pursue. When each commits his or her thoughts to paper, it is seen that combining advice gives the best possible path. Two partners in a firm think they have differences that are not really there, once they are clearly defined.

Meaning: Clear definition of a problem results in good luck. A new path defined by two elderly men is indicated.

6–6: The ultimate good fortune. No matter what you do, you will be successful. You cannot avoid gaining wealth—unexpected wealth, such as the winning of a lottery.

Meaning: Anything you touch turns to gold. Lucky good fortune.

Blank-1: The Void can support nothing.[3] Even the great energy of 1 will eventually be absorbed by It. An extra effort may enable the subject to overcome the background that tries to pull him or her down. Loss and illness are likely.

Meaning: Extraordinary efforts are required to avoid failure. Look for unexpected health problems.

1-Blank: In striving upward, 1's efforts are muffled by the Void. If a minister, this denotes success as an evangelist or a missionary far from home; but usually a path around should be found.

Meaning: Attack the problem vigorously from a new angle. If a minister, travel.

Blank-2: This person is not concerned about falling backward. He or she has little concern that the background is a void; but must take great care not to fall into the pit. If the fire is lost, all is lost.

Meaning: Preserve your energy. Go forward. Do not care what people say about your background.

2-Blank: Sexual energy can absorb the blank. The opinion of others regarding your actions must be ignored. You will marry a missionary.

Meaning: The future looks bleak, but you can go forward and be successful if you make sexual overtures to a religious person.

Blank-3: 3's persistent small steps take you surely across the Void. You will lose ground as you cross, but you will still come out the other side.

---

[3]The number given first is considered to be toward the left of the reader.

Meaning: Prepare for some setbacks. Persistence in doing the things you know brings success.

3-Blank: 3 is being held down by the Void (in this case unknown problems)—but hardly notices. In a boring, yet persistent, way you will continue to plod on until the Void goes away. You will scrupulously attend church though you believe you are a sinner but it won't bother you very much.

Meaning: Some problems are ahead, but don't worry. Be persistent and they will go away.

Blank-4: The mature person finds support in religion or in contemplation of the afterlife. You draw strength from your intuitive understanding of the meaning of life.

Meaning: There are hidden problems you must understand before you can proceed. Take nothing for granted.

4-Blank: The mature person's head is in the clouds. You are so involved in the church that your family suffers. Everything must be given up and subordinated to your church-going activities. You find great satisfaction in these activities, whereas those around you suffer.

Meaning: Don't worry about vague undefined problems and promises. Reliance on what you know for a fact brings success.

Blank-5: The old man's faith is threatened. He discovers something which means that the basis of his wisdom is questionable. Unless he is careful, he will fall totally into introspection and self-doubt.

Meaning: Look carefully at your basic assumptions. Is the marketing forecast valid? Is the envisioned partner truly as he or she has represented himself? Wishes are not horses.

5-Blank: The philosopher is off on a trip of his own into philosophical realms that few can understand and where few can follow. His head is firmly in the clouds. His views are colored by his withdrawal from the mundane world.

Meaning: Do not follow apparently altruistic advice from an older person. You live in the mundane world and must suffer the consequences.

Blank-6: The All-Mother in her wisdom has the spiritual world at her feet. She intuitively understands it. It presents no danger to her; she can draw inspiration from it. She increases her wealth and prosperity by following her intuitive hunches and knowledge.

Meaning: Following the inexplicable hunch of an older person, especially a woman, brings great success.

6-Blank: Opposites combine. Heaven and earth encompass all that is between them. No matter what enterprise is contemplated, whether it be mining or opening a spiritual retreat, it will succeed; for the All-Mother and heaven are in balance and agreement.

Meaning: Go ahead. Success is yours.

1-2: This is the most unstable combination in the set of tiles. He is obsessed with bedding her; she is obsessed with keeping him down and under control. The Sword can be tempered in the Fire, but the Fire is always on top. The situation cannot continue.

Meaning: Frustration. Imminent collapse of an endeavor.

2-1: Stability, with the creativity of the Fire urging the tempered Sword to greater efforts. Beware of being sucked dry. At every turn she urges him on. She is the Fury who urges the young willing man into battle.

Meaning: Great success from creative endeavors that do not overreach themselves, especially in the creation of new shapes and new things in metal that has to be heated.

1-3: Although there is instability inherent in this relationship, so long as 3 can control the creative urges and upward thrusts of 1, good can come from it. It is tricky and is likely to blow up at any time. The company executives have to train and mold younger men; the balance between giving them their head and keeping a tight rein is critical to success of the venture.

Meaning: For success, great care must be exercised regarding the control of younger people.

3-1: 1 is on top. The situation is stable as long as 3 is the steadfast rock on which 1 stands. It is the positive combination of opposites. This is a particularly fortunate tile when 1 is willing to accept some guidance from 3.

Meaning: Go ahead; but for success, seek advice from an older, more stable friend or employee.

1-4: The activities of the eldest son are absorbed by the matron. Yet, although now she controls him, she can feel that he will break away from home very soon. She knows she cannot keep him under her forever.

Meaning: Unstable relationships. A dissolution of a long-standing partnership. Loss through deceit. If the relationship (being read) is of a young man and an older woman, he is interested in her money.

4-1: Creative urges are encouraged. He is being positively pushed out into the world. Provided he remembers his loving mother, he will be successful.

Meaning: Creativity modified by mother-love brings success.

1-5: The Sage has a young thrusting neophyte to teach and to lead. The Sage reduces his advice to writing and overcomes the neophyte's sword-like thrusts; for, as the saying has it, the Word is mightier than the Sword.

Meaning: A troublesome opponent becomes a supporter when threatened with a lawsuit.

5–1: The old man proudly presents his creative son to the world. He is blind to the boy's faults and will support him far longer than he should. The son causes problems and the old man has to write many letters. Seeing his son's ambition and creativity pleases the Sage. If the boy is too obstreperous, the Sage should push him toward a career in the armed forces.

Meaning: Too long supporting one who should be maturing brings misfortune. Give the problem to some large organization, even if doing so means that a jail term will follow.

1–6: This tile shows partial instability. Grandmother has an influence over the son that nothing can disturb. Her influence may wax and wane, but it will always be there. She exercises it partially through careful use of her mundane wealth. While he is under her, his creative urges are momentarily stilled. A temporary rest is indicated here, a time of relaxation from more violent creative activities. He is under the protection of the All-Mother.

Meaning: A temporary lull before further creative efforts.

6–1: Grandmother sends her creative, energetic son into the world with all the support she can muster. He can draw from the well of her knowledge, understanding, and wealth; and the well will supply him endlessly with what he needs.

Meaning: Good fortune and success come to those who rely on the resources of an older woman.

2–3: This is the typical relationship between the staid businessman and his young ambitious secretary, the fiery redhead. If she does not seduce him, and if he can get her to admire him, the apparently unstable relationship can bring great success to both; for he will make president of the firm and she will become the chief executive's secretary. Her fire heats his stone but does not break it.

Meaning: Do not succumb to a lustful temptation. Success comes through emotional control.

3-2: The Fire has seduced the stone. She burns brightly with the stone beneath her. This may be the spendthrift wayward wife with the adoring blind husband, or it may be the all-consuming passion of a business enterprise that is actually a losing proposition.

Meaning: Dump the woman and come to your senses. Sell off the losing flashy product line.

2-4: The matron understands, and by ignoring it dims the flame of the ambitious craftswoman. Water puts out the Fire. There is a controversy here, but it is controversy that is largely ignored. Steam is generated but quickly dissipates into the air. This is not a positive tile, for it shows the unthinking rejection of new crafts and ideas.

Meaning: Misfortune comes through the rejection of a new idea.

4-2: The foundation of maturity enables the fiery young craftswoman to succeed. The Fire burns on the lake. Provided the craftswoman keeps moving, the lake will support her. If she stops, she will be overcome and her fire lost in the lake.

Meaning: Success comes through the dispassionate support of new ideas.

2-5: The unstable relationship between an old man and a young girl. The Sage is burned at the fire of desire. The relationship will break apart, either when he dies or when she has milked him for everything she can get.

Meaning: Trouble is brewing. People around you can see that you are being very foolish.

5-2: The Sage in his wisdom supports his daughter. Although he does not necessarily approve, he can understand her sexuality and can be amused still by her foibles. This is often a joyful, happy tile; and with care the relationship can lead to success.

Meaning: Watch and enjoy the play of life, but do not get involved.

2-6: The Earth envelops the Fire. No matter what the young girl does, grandmother is understanding and shelters her. Her energy can be lost in the old woman's placidity; but if she keeps within her own bounds, the young woman's craft can flower. The light is temporarily sheltered under the bushel.

Meaning: Confined craft activity will bring success.

6-2: Volcano — The Fire springs from the Earth. Nothing can stand in its way. If it is controlled and directed by the Earth, it is not unduly destructive. This is the most powerful female creation tile, for islands are created in the sea and new land appears where there was none before. When it is held down, a destructive explosion will result. When given free rein, it can appear very beautiful.

Meaning: Going forward freely brings success. Repressing impulses leads to disaster.

3-4: The matron has slight ascendancy over her husband. Small conflicts will easily be resolved. Water flows over Stone and cools and suppresses some of its desires and ambitions; but the repression is gentle, not dramatic. Disagreements will be resolved quietly, not destructively or very creatively, for that matter.

Meaning: Moderate success comes through the settlement of small disagreements.

4-3: In the Western world, this tile represents the natural relationship of the stable family. The rather boring hardworking man is supported by his happy wife. She has some depth upon which he can draw, though the supply is not inexhaustible. Unless modern thought intrudes, there is no disagreement here.

Meaning: Continued work and the conservation of resources brings moderate serenity and success. Stay with old-fashioned products.

3-5: The grandfather overwhelms his son and keeps him down. There is mild conflict here. The situation will not last forever, though it may last a lot longer than it should. If it continues, all originality will be extinguished in the younger man.

Meaning: A business that is set in its ways should make innovations and retire the old fogeys.

5-3: The father supports his son. Success comes through the older man's support and recognition of the younger man's stability and devotion to work. Success is great in matters of earned wealth and commerce; success will not come through modern creative ideas. This is a good solid relationship. The business is stable because it is a sound legal entity that keeps exact and precise books. It is happy to pay its taxes and to be regarded as an old-line solid family concern.

Meaning: Success comes through persistence and strengthening of ties between older and younger members of the family. Commit everything to writing.

3-6: The Stone is in its natural place under the Earth. The Earth can be plowed without any danger of breaking the equipment. By the hard-working support of the young man, the wealthy grandmother has great good fortune. Occasionally there is a negative connotation of instability here, especially in relationships where an old woman takes a gigolo to bed. This is the gigolo one should beware of, for he appears in a conservative middle-aged guise. In business it can appear to be a very worth-while venture, but there are hidden dangers; for the old woman does not see the gigolo's faults.

Meaning: Success comes through continually plowing the old ground. Avoid a new venture that seems to have promise, especially if presented by a possessive middle-aged man.

6–3: Grandmother supports her eldest son. He can draw on her wealth and experience to further his business. Stability and success are indicated, provided the support is not rejected.

Meaning: Success through using the resources of older people.

4–5: The young matron supports her grandfather. This is a tile of success when it refers to the mature woman supporting the older man in a commercial business venture. It is especially successful in cases of lawyers. He can draw on her small reserves and this is all he needs to succeed. The relationship is stable because he does not harass her sexually. He does not demand obedience, and she is mature enough to get her way without quarrels.

Meaning: Success comes through reliance on a mature woman. Relationships will last, provided no attempt is made to wreak violent change on an older man's set ways.

5–4: One of the most stable relationships in the tiles. This tile can even indicate marriage. Two older people with the woman slightly younger join together in a venture. He supports her actions and she relies on his careful abilities to reduce everything to writing to make sure that her every step is on firm ground.

Meaning: Proceed surely and steadily, and success will be yours. Marry the man.

4–6: This is a stable tile, though some frustration and conflict are shown. The younger woman wishes to learn from the older, but does not wish to be entirely taken over and enveloped by her. The younger woman must make her own freedom in a limited fashion so she does not upset the stability of the older woman.

Meaning: Success lies in rejecting attempts at engulfing moves. Maintain your autonomy.

6-4: The grandmother supports her mature daughter, who can draw on the grandmother's wealth to succeed in new fields associated with her previous knowledge. She must maintain close ties to her roots. If she goes off with wild new endeavors, she breaks the tie and misfortune is hers.

Meaning: Success comes through new endeavors based on old skills, lines of business, friends, and family.

5-6: The most stable tile in the entire set. The elderly woman gently controls the old man. If he is a philosopher, she translates his mystic meanings into words the world can understand. This good tile encourages marriages between old friends and more elderly people. It shows great success through commercial endeavors.

Meaning: Continue to pursue your stable path. A joining together of two older enterprises. A marriage is beneficial.

6-5: The Sage is supported by the elderly woman. He can draw on her reserves and wealth to make the world a better place. His writings and sayings change the lives of thousands if not millions of people. If the writings are good, the changes are good; but the contrary can also be true.

Meaning: Success comes through wide distribution of written material.

Time Sequence Readings

After the basic reading, a time-sequence reading can be done for a period of 7 days, 7 weeks, 7 months, or 7 years. The subject chooses seven tiles, each representing one of the chosen time units, and places them end to end face down before the reader. The present starts at the reader's left, and time periods move into the future toward her right. She turns up one tile at a time by standing the tile on its long side and letting it fall face up.

●   ●   ●

Traditionally the dominoes should be kept in a worn candy or tobacco can which is battered and dented with nearly all its paint worn or scraped off. The tin is said to keep unwanted vibrations out of the tiles, and its hoary age is said to show the wisdom that has been drawn out of the tiles in time past. As with all methods of divination, a little mystery helps; and the more emotion you can generate in the subject, and the more involved the client becomes, the more accurate will be the outcome.

Chapter 5

Dice Divination

"Snake eyes!" What could indicate bad luck more clearly? "Box cars!" The double-6 obviously spells good fortune to anyone. Most of us, not being regular craps players, are not able to judge the significance of 7's and 11's; but for centuries when the die (as individual dice are called) has been cast, people have relied on the roll of these little ivory cubes to indicate what fate had in store for them. Since the traditional methods have been taken up by gamblers, their forecast meanings have become overshadowed by the carnival atmosphere of Las Vegas and other gambling centers. The work of Professor J. B. Rhine and Mrs. Rhine at Duke University seems to indicate that the fall of the dice can be influenced by the mind, even when the dice are rolled by a randomizing machine.

We all recognize that the mind can actually influence mechanical objects, but in some of the Rhine experiments we cannot tell whether success was due to this psychokinetic effect or a prediction on the part of the operator as to what the results would be. In trials where emphasis was placed on making a specified number come up, it is clear that psychokinesis was at work.

Setting Up

In the pubs of England, the favorite pastime is the game of darts. Many times after closing time and several calls "Drink up, gentlemen!" from the bar, the dart board was taken down and dice cast upon it. Often these casts were done to figure out who was going to win the next football or cricket match. With its many numbers, its bullseye, its doubles and triples, the dart board made an ideal predictive baseboard. The wires on its surface and the scarred irregularities caused by the impact of the darts made the dice roll and come to rest in unpredictable ways, sometimes even to balance on edge. The best we can do to simulate a baseboard of this type is to use a coarse burlap and mark on it the pattern shown in figure 18. Cut a piece of 1/4" exterior plywood in a perfect circle with a diameter of 23". Stretch the burlap over it and glue it in place. Varnish the surface. Then draw on it the pattern shown in fig. 17 (page 60) exercising extreme care to get it drawn and colored as precisely as possible. Although the surface will not have the roughness or the protrusions of the dart board, it still brings the possibilities and combinations up into the range of the many millions that a good predictive method needs.

The old dice-throwers owned their own dice for many years; they knew from the peculiarities of each die which one represented the subject and which ones represented (for example) a close friend or business interests. Since you will be starting with new dice instead of dice you have owned for years, it is good to obtain them in different colors. White, brown, and black are readily available. We use white for the subject, brown for the close friend, and black for business or money aspects of the question.

The reader always throws the dice; the subject never does, although the subject is often allowed to shake them in their wooden cup. Sometimes the dice fall within the pattern of the board; but at other times they fall outside, or "away." The numbers the dice show, together with the number of the segment and the color they fall on, are all significant.

Traditionally the reader becomes very agitated when he or she shakes the dice in their wooden cup, and yells some mystical word to awaken the consciousness at the instant the dice are cast. The word should be meaningless in everyday terms. "Abracadabra" is often used, and Sybil Leek recommended "Ah-Dah-Dee-Err!" The exact word is not so important as its volume. We have seen people let off cap pistols, strike a gong, and even break glassware at the instant of the dice throw. Loudness and shock value seem to be what is required.

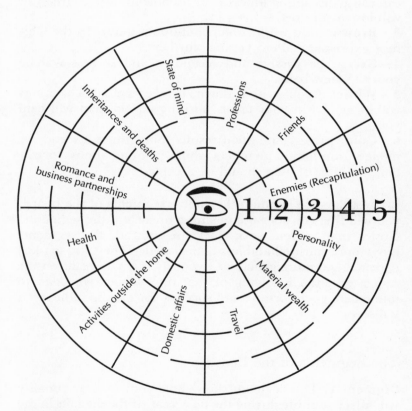

Figure 18. Dice casting baseboard. Numbers refer to annular ring colors. See Table 6 on page 86.

Individual Dice Numbers

The meanings of these numbers are similar to those shown by individual domino numbers; this is obviously because the two predictive methods share a common source.

1 — Blue: male, thrusting creativity. A telegram or a telephone call will bring news of an opportunity.
2 — Red: beware the sexy, fiery redheaded female, for she can cause disruption unless your friendships are secure. You will lose a sure bet.
3 — Brown: hard work, small continuous gains. In the Chinese expression, "Perseverance furthers."
4 — Green: be passive and receptive, and success will be yours. A new baby.
5 — White: if you write it down, or get legal advice, things will be settled in your favor. Visiting an old man will help you.
6 — Gold: success and good results. Sometimes a legacy or money from family members whom you had almost forgotten. An offer of help should be accepted.

As the dice fall onto the twelve segments of the board, you will first consider the meaning of each of the segments. Notice that as you work clockwise around, the segments grow more spiritual and less materialistic. They also get less personal and more general. Obviously if any die falls on the center eye, the following of that die's advice will lead to immediate good fortune and success, for the die indicates a bullseye.

The Segments of the Board

Segment 1: This segment shows how your own personality will affect your life during the next year. If the die falls in the red segment, there will be travel and activity; if it falls in the yellow segment, it indicates an improvement in fortunes and the harvesting of something that will bring you more wealth — the payment of an old debt, the gathering in of a crop. In green, you must look carefully for hidden problems in the area under consideration. The subject should not make any major decisions in the forthcoming year without carefully studying them. Blue indicates that good fortune will arrive through hard continuous work. As the die falls more toward the outside rim of the board, meanings tend toward a more manual nature. Black has its own meaning of death. Depending which die falls here and how it falls, it can be the death of hope or the death of a close friend.

Segment 2: This segment shows how the subject's material wealth will be affected by the topic under review. If the die falls in the red segment, there will be many ups and downs — much activity, but little gain. The subject might get a job one week that pays a lot, and be out of work the next. If the die falls in the yellow section, there will be great gain and good success. If it falls in the green, investments should be considered. If in the blue, hard manual work brings good fortune. If in the black, as the Chinese would say, "Nothing furthers." It doesn't matter what the subject does, nothing will bring in a larger income at this time.

Segment 3: This segment relates specifically to travel and whether travel will or will not be beneficial. The segment can also be called separation; that is, when someone feels he or she is in love, travel is indicated so that a cooling-off period between the lovers can be allowed. If the die falls in the red section, lots of travel on short, quick journeys is indicated. If in the yellow, travel is very beneficial. In the green, travel to the mountains is a must. In the blue, travel across an ocean; but a fall in the black indicates that the subject should stay home.

Segment 4: This relates to domestic affairs and to the private life of the subject. A die in the red indicates separation, divorce, or the subject leaving home. In the yellow, all is sunny and bright, with much happiness. In the green, a new baby is clearly indicated. In the blue, much renovation, repainting, especially rehabilitation of an old building brings success. Black here is a warning sign of the most ominous sort. It presages destruction and the end. The subject should look to his or her insurance.

Segment 5: This segment shows activities outside the home, and the way people perceive them. If the die falls in the red, the subject will be perceived as unreliable and almost spastic in his or her frantic activities. "He never has time fer nuthin'," is a typical judgment about this type of person. In the yellow, the subject is likable but always waiting for money. Occasionally there is great success, but it should be expected only every nine months or so. In green, outside activities in the fields of commerce and teaching are successful. In other fields, the subject is regarded as a bookworm — full of theory, not very practical. Blue indicates the good, honest, hard-working person; black indicates the lazy slob.

Segment 6: This segment shows health and vitality. If the die falls in red, the subject has a great deal of nervous energy but can be very brittle and in the long run not dependable. The subject is worried about physical health, and looks after himself or herself very well. In yellow, the radiant athletic good health that everyone would love to enjoy if it weren't so much trouble. Green has a duality of meaning: it can mean the plump person who cares more for spiritual ideas than for health; or it can mean the thin, stoop-shouldered aesthetic type who worries so little about nutrition that health suffers. Green is not a color of good health; but the cause of the ill health can be anything from carelessness in diet to eating too much. In black we find the rugged hard-working square-looking person. At first glance he or she appears overweight, but then you realize it's all muscle — and all in good condition. Here black becomes its most ominous. The subject has nine days in which to get medical attention.

Segment 7: This segment reads romance and business partnerships. Why these two fall together in this type of divination system is unclear; perhaps business partnerships were not a common thing among pub-goers. The romance of getting into business or being romanced by someone who wants the subject's money is the concern here. The readings tend to be earthy — as befits their origin, where the farmyard and the bed were closer to the living quarters than they are nowadays. Red indicates a lot of sex, but no results; that is, no conceptions. A lot of talk about a business or possible ventures, but none are started. Yellow indicates a long, long romance with a very gradual approach to consummation. The long chaste engagement: the couple are happy to walk hand in hand; but (much to the amusement of the community) nothing ever happens. Green is the most positive color in these relationships, for it indicates balance and a new creation. The partners are joined, and their actions have created something new. Blue shows a working partnership flowering into marriage. Many children result. In business, a good solid idea that requires physical labor brings great success. Black says, "Don't get romantically entangled; don't get a little bit pregnant; stay in the shadows and watch."

Segment 8: This area shows inheritance and deaths. Red means much promised, little fulfilled. The subject is put in someone's will — but nobody dies. Yellow indicates a family member that the subject has known for a long time dies and leaves much wealth. Green indicates money comes from an unexpected death, probably overseas. At least it is from a source of which the subject has no knowledge or close connections. Blue says this is the money that comes from father's death or from the person the subject would prefer had lived. Typically the recipient would rather go on working for or with the decedent than have the fortune. Black here becomes its most positive. There are no deaths — and consequently no inheritances.

Segment 9: This shows state of mind. For a young subject, it can also be construed as advice on educational matters. The die in the red indicates a light-weight thinker with the lightning mind, a witty pun-maker at the party whom one dislikes because only later can one think of a rapier comeback. In education, it indicates the subject should be a generalist and take up several subjects rather than specializing. In yellow, the intelligent person's success comes through careful mental evaluation of a problem. In education, the subject should continue to work for higher and higher qualifications in the disciplines he or she likes. Green means unexpected thoughts; unexpected insights are indicated, probably through contact with someone of the opposite gender. In education it is a pushing toward philosophy. Blue shows the subject who has to think hard and long about any problem. Sometimes, indeed, the subject thinks so long and hard that he or she does nothing. This mind is very resistant to new ideas. In education, it indicates that a solid base of the three R's is required, and that the subject would be better off getting a practical education than one befitting a thinker. Black means that no more education is required; no matter how long the subject studies this problem, it isn't going to get any better. To fix it, the subject will have to do something in a practical way.

Segment 10: This area indicates the professions and businesses that the subject should consider. Red—travel, sport, and the armed services are indicated. Yellow—physician, public-relations work, row-crop farming. Green—market gardening, minister, teacher. Blue—any manual labor. The closer to the center of the board the die falls, the more craft will be the labor (in the sense of craftsmanship). Sometimes subjects recoil at readings that urge menial labor; but the way things are going in this world, there will very soon be a complete dearth of those who can work with their hands. Then the old English saying, "Where there's muck there's money," will never have been more true. The least-favored occupation for this group is that of animal husbandry, especially the raising of hogs; yet it is the most rewarding. Black—no professional or business changes or decisions should be made. The subject is as well off here for the next nine months as he or she would be anywhere.

Segment 11: Friends. With the die in red, the subject has many very shallow friendships with few moments of intense emotion attached to them. Petty jealousy and hate occur too often. These are not true friends; they are only acquaintances. Yellow — the subject has many childhood friends still near with whom he or she corresponds and communicates. These are true friends, supportive through problems. At the present time the subject should rely on them. Green — a weird collection of friends in many places. The network of friends extends from people in high places to those who work in the sewers. Many of them live in distant lands, yet the subject can still count them as friends — and they reciprocate. Because of these far-ranging friendships, the subject can help other people with contacts, but is unable to use friends to help himself or herself. For the friends would feel used; and although they would oblige the first time, they would no longer be friends thereafter. Blue — friends from college days and from the days when the subject cruised the town. The subject is a club member, a strong union type, who finds strength in numbers. Black — friendless and withdrawn. The subject must go out — at whatever cost — and make a few friends.

Segment 12: Although this segment traditionally regards enemies, we like to read it as an indicator of the outcome or the wrap-up. Red — there will be trouble, arguments, and disagreements before a resolution is found. Red is indicative of war. Yellow — great success. There are some difficulties that are overcome harmoniously; but success is definitely ahead. Green — beware the unknown, the spy, the enemy, the police informer. There is something about the deal the subject doesn't know. Be very wary. Make sure that when the subject finds out what is wrong that it really is what is wrong. There may be secrets within secrets. Blue — back to the Chinese: "Perseverance furthers." Hard work brings small but continued good fortune. Black — deepest mysteries. If they are not solved, they may led to the death of hopes, relationships, and even to a funeral; yet if the mysteries are solved the outcome will be very favorable.

Table 5. Meanings of Dice Numbers

Number	Meaning	Color
1	Male, thrusting, creative	Blue
2	Red-headed sexy female temptress	Red
3	Hard worker	Brown
4	Passive receptor	Green
5	Lawyer	White
6	Money, success	Gold

Table 6. Meanings of Ring Colors

Color	Number	Meaning
Black	5	Death; the Void
Blue	4	Hard work
Green	3	Study; new beginnings
Yellow	2	Sunshine; continue on path
Red	1	Fragile, fiery

Table 5 summarizes the basic meanings of the various numbers. Table 6 summarizes the meanings of the colors on the board. If you can memorize these tables, plus the meanings of the segments as shown in fig. 18 on page 79, you will be a long way toward having great success as a dice diviner.

The Away Dice

More often than you might think, the dice fall outside the burlap circle onto the incidental background. These away dice, as they are called, have great significance.

One away: indicates a disruption of plans within the week — a new direction. The totals of the dice remaining inside the circle must be examined for the area from which the new direction will come.

Two away: almost immediately, certainly within a week, there will be a quarrel. Sybil Leek, who had not (shall we say) the most placid temperament imaginable, said that the quarrel would often occur between the reader and the subject: the subject would accuse the reader of stupidity, drunkenness, and other frailties. The position of the die within the circle is important in ascertaining the root of the quarrel.

Three away: all is not lost, for the subject's wishes will be met. Often that wish is for the dice to be thrown again. If the subject has expressed no wish, he or she is told to make a wish immediately. In some social groups, a loud demand is made that the reader buy another round of drinks!

Meaning of the Totals within the Circle

We have examined the significance of the numbers showing on the faces of the dice between 1 and 6. Those meanings are to be used for evaluating both the meaning of a single die lying within a segment, and the added total of the numbers showing on all the dice cast. Numbers 1 and 2 occur very rarely in the totals; but when some dice are away, they can and do occur and are at their most powerful. It is often good to think of the colors of the numbers as they fall within the colors of the circle segments; for in this way you can see contrasts and parallels more quickly.

Additional Meanings of Totals of All the Dice

7 — Brown: This indicates difficulties along the path. It represents a businessman who is not necessarily friendly, as typified by the stereotypical rent collector. If the subject can pay, he is happy and jovial and presents no problems. Make sure the subject has enough reserves to overcome what fate may throw.

8 — Black: Two strong women are very critical. If the subject can withstand their criticism, he or she will win through to good fortune. The criticism is not necessarily valid. It can come from someone spreading unfounded rumors about the subject. Because of the criticism, be very careful in changing direction. Divide and conquer. Walk straight down the path between the two women, and all will be well.

9 — Lavender: Good clothes and pretty things displayed with good taste show a marriage. The marriage is not the first for either partner, and new things will not be created in it; but the alliance will bring much happiness and it will last a long time.

10 — Pale green: This is a new baby, the birth of a new idea, or the mind's awakening to an old idea which is now seen in a completely new light. It is pale because unless the idea is carefully tended, it will never grow to fruition. With care a great harvest will be reaped.

11 — Turquoise: Parting and return. Two people will go their separate ways, but will come back to each other and make violent love. Friendship after parting results in a strong marriage.

12 — Orange: The subject will receive news of good fortune. Maybe the hospital tests all turned out negative, or the subject won a lottery or sweepstakes, or someone left money. The news is communicated by letter instead of more quickly by telephone or telegram.

13 — Gray: Something hidden catches up with the subject from the past. It may even mean that he or she must go to jail; but in general it is the result of some past action that makes the subject feel guilty and sorrowful. It is good that the problem is straightened out.

14 — Amber: A new golden friendship of a purely platonic nature, often with an older person, will bring success in the very near future. A small business is absorbed by an old firm, and both gain from it.

15 — Day-glow red: Stop. Back up. Caution. Be very careful of anything done in the next few days. Be especially cautious for the next 9 hours, and for the next 9 days. Avoid travel, and test each step on a stairway before putting full weight on it. Do not climb ladders or go up scaffolding.

16 — Pink: At the end of a long journey the subject finds a blushing maiden or a reward. Something that has been kept sheltered from his or her gaze, always partially hidden, reveals itself; and with its help or its use, great fortune will come.

17 — Beige or natural tan: A change of plans results from a change in the basic background information that has been given. It all happens harmoniously. Nothing sudden, startling, or unexpected occurs. New information comes and the subject is easily able to accept it; from this comes a change of plans which harmoniously brings moderate success.

18 — Gold: No matter what the subject does, he or she has the Midas touch. Money will come in great gobs. The rashest investment brings a good return. But be careful and look where the dice fall; for perhaps the money will flow away just as quickly as it came.

In many ways interpretation of dice takes a better memory than does any other form of prediction. When casting the dice, there is also a great temptation to make many throws. This must not happen. A single throw, or at the most two, when in the first throw 3 dice were away, should be made on any question. Longer contemplation of the pattern, longer discussion of the meanings with the subject, result in better readings than does the making of several throws on the same question. The combinations are infinite. It is very rare that one of the dice does not fall on a dividing line between two segments or is partially in one color sector but mainly in another. This immediately gives a percentage feeling for the influences involved. If you take the die representing the subject and consider that each sector has only 5 segments, if the die were to fall cleanly in the very center of each colored sector on the first reading there would be 360 basic meanings. When you put in 3 dice and consider the possible combinations, you can see that millions upon millions of variations are possible, and that as the dice move across the sectors fine shadings and differentiations multiply.

Because of the many variables and the memory work involved, we recommend you try a few rehearsal passes at home before you venture out into the arena of doing readings for others. Whatever you do, let your CC have full play as you view the board; for that is why this type of divination is so spectacularly successful.

Chapter 6

Astromancy

"Sacrilege! Heresy! Burn 'em at the stake!" Dedicated, mathematically oriented astrologers should quit reading now, because, one more time, we will be kicking some sacred cows. The popularity of astrology has never been higher. More people know their sun sign than ever before. Yet we do not currently see any startling predictions coming true as they did in the past. It is our belief that the Consciousness Connection plays more of a part in predictions from astrological charts than most astrologers will admit.

In some 2,000 charts calculated over the years for a single nativity by students at our School (many of whom were making their first attempt at calculating a chart), gross errors crept in. Some 20 percent of the charts wound up being more than four hours off, and more than 50 percent were at least half an hour off. Astrologers say that the birth time must be correct in order to calculate a chart and make accurate predictions. Yet by and large our predictions (at least 90 percent of them) were correct because the students had been instructed to meditate on the charts rather than looking up answers in textbooks. We also purchased 20 computer analyses for the same nativity, and although the computer had fewer mathematical errors, fully three quarters (75 percent) disagreed with the predictions of the great body of our students. Three charts were calculated by professional astrologers; one was calculated correctly, one was also four hours off, and one had no longitudinal correction (making it, in this case, several minutes off). Yet all three professional charts agreed exactly with the predictions made by the majority of our students! It is clear, therefore, that charts and analyses prepared by computers and by rigid adherence to textbooks are missing the point. Astrology cannot be reduced to a simple exercise in mathematics; the Consciousness Connection must be allowed to play its part.

We also note that astrological prediction seemed to work better in the past than it does now; but when people with developed psychic ability use even traditional methods, they are able to get good predictions whether or not they get the numbers right.

In this section we will not work with the mathematics of astrology. You computer types can switch off, for we are going analog. Not only that, but our meters are going to read feelings, and hence are not going to be precisely calibrated. We are teachers, not astrologers. Gavin has an advanced degree in mathematics; he once taught celestial navigation in the real world, the world where death results from errors. We have found that without the angel of death sitting on their shoulder, few people indeed can calculate a chart with great accuracy; but we have also found that given the basic sun sign and perhaps a few more pieces of information (such as the rising sun), most people with any CC at all can accurately predict. We promise strictly to limit our discussion of astrology's technical aspects so we can make this more of a fun exercise.

Our View of the Signs

The traditional descriptions of birth signs are sadly outdated. Oh, the basic ideas behind the analyses are right enough; but the sign details are so askew that we are going to take the whole art and shake it up to come out with new definitions. Because we teach so many students, and because we don't go gaga when someone tells us that Grand Poobah N____ says it should be so, we will explain to you what the signs mean to us and to the thousands of people whom we have taught.

First of all, we object to using animal metaphors to explain a personality, to take a personality out of the human framework. That animal metaphor is far too one-dimensional ever to be satisfactory. What we are going to do is help you put those one-dimensional metaphors back into a framework of living, breathing human beings. Each framework is formed around a nucleus family. Some of its members are rather flaky, and others may seem exaggerated caricatures, but at least they are real people. When you put them into a situation you can imagine how they will react.

We retain the traditional astrological concepts of fire, earth, air, water (the elements) as shown in the coloring of each family member. Astrologers also work with the terms cardinal, fixed, and mutable to describe certain sign categories. We don't like these words either. We have found that the word cardinal has little or no meaning to students. In general usage it means a fixed point, like the cardinal points of a compass, or a person who has been set in authority, like a cardinal in the Roman Catholic Church. The cardinal water sign of conventional astrology is Cancer. But the attributes of the sign are not related to a compass point or to a position of authority. No more resemblance is found in fixed or mutable signs to their adjectives. We tend to think of cardinal signs as reliable in the sense of always being there, instead of in the sense of behaving predictably. Fixed and mutable signs bear little relation to those words.

Our Astrological Family

Look now at figure 19 on page 94 and the rather large family group. These are very human people. To avoid too much confusion, we will use the traditional names for the dates of birth traditionally assigned; for readers unfamiliar with the dates, Table 7 on page 95 lists them.

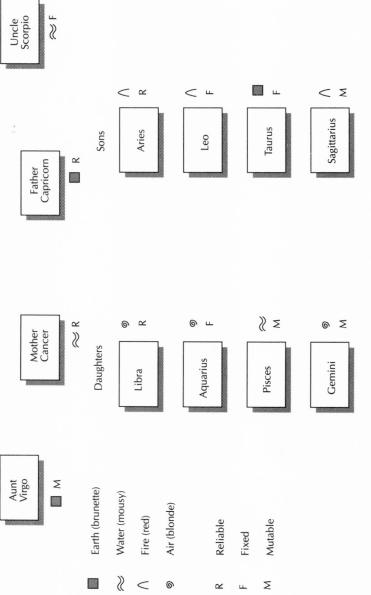

Figure 19. Astrological family members.

Mother Cancer: She owns a stone house in the country by a lake. She is overweight and often seems disorganized; but after mothering nine children, she has the right to be a little untidy. She never has time to buy new clothes, but instead wears the same outfit for a long time and then discards it. She is very sympathetic, but often unpunctual. She would rather stay home and look after the family than keep a series of tight business appointments. Mother always has her hands in water, washing something. Being short, plump, and bulgy, she gives an impression of softness, though occasionally she does lash out, especially when her home or her

Table 7. Nativity dates for family members.*

Sign	Color	Dates
Mother Cancer	Amber	June 21–July 22
Father Capricorn	Indigo	December 22–January 19
Uncle Scorpio	Brown	October 23–November 21
Aunt Virgo	Chartreuse	August 23–September 22
Eldest Son Aries	Scarlet	March 21–April 19
Eldest Daughter Libra	Emerald	September 23–October 22
Second Son Leo	Gold	July 23–August 22
Second Daughter Aquarius	Violet	January 20–February 18
Third Son Taurus	Red	April 20–May 20
Third Daughter Pisces	Lavender	February 19–March 20
Youngest Son Sagittarius	Blue	November 22–December 21
Youngest Daughters Gemini	Yellow	May 21–June 20

*South of the Equator, add six months.

family is threatened. Everyone runs to her with their problems — but no one can tell what she is thinking. She has untidy, faintly blond hair, and amber eyes.

Father Capricorn: With his dark blue suit and neatly brushed hair, dear old hard-working Papa is the ideal mate for Mother Cancer. As head of the family, he feels duty-bound to see that nothing goes to waste. Every broken toy that was ever bought has been recycled. He knows where every dollar was spent; he is so serious that through his lack of understanding his daughters, he has not been able to communicate with them and they have turned out rather badly by his standards. The girls think he is something of a dry old stick, and in fact he is humorless. But because he cannot bring himself to be punitive, they get away with murder. Old Papa has high ideals for himself and often worries that he is not meeting his own standards.

Uncle Scorpio: Uncle shares his brother's lack of humor on the surface, but to compensate for that he enjoys all the good things of the world. He is a little careless about his attire; he's the one with ring around the collar. Though plump, he has more determination than is expected from someone who would be called fat by current standards. His large red beard is turning gray, and he seems to hide behind it; for he is always thinking, always scheming his schemes. While talking with one person, he seems able to follow other conversations and simultaneously plot traps for the unwary. The girls like him, for he tends to be bawdy; but they have learned to hold his hands while they talk with him. He can even coax a rare smile from Aunt Virgo. He wears turquoise jewelry and brown clothing.

Aunt Virgo: She is Mother's spinster sister. Tall, thin, a beanpole of a woman with dark long hair that seems to accentuate her prim expression, she dresses like a 70-year-old crusader for chastity. Her small closed mouth and folded hands betray her disapproval of most things that go on in the household. She especially tries to correct her sister's slapdash ways, and is still trying vainly to get all the girls to go to church with her. As a young woman Aunt made a lot of money with a chain of stores her father left her. Occasionally she wears a chartreuse gown and goes off to a good restaurant with Uncle Scorpio. She is shy and retiring, though the girls regularly get together to take her out; and any time she starts weeding the garden, someone is sure to come to help her.

Aries: The eldest son—Ari has neatly trimmed hair of dark red; he always appears well dressed even though some of his clothes are old. He is tall and slender, and wears the slightly harried expression of the eldest son, the experimental model, the one who is responsible for all the younger siblings. He has never been really sick a day in his life; he is conscious of diet and sometimes angers his mother by rejecting the more fattening of her dishes. He works as a layout artist at the offices of a women's magazine. There his quiet persistent sexuality makes him successful with many ladies who visit the offices; though few in the family, including the sisters, realize how many notches there really are on his headboard. He is secretive, and values himself above all others.

Libra: Libby, the eldest daughter—the darkest blond of all the girls. She is tall and something of a beauty. Between her beauty and her affectionate, loving nature, she is continually in trouble with her father and her aunt; for they are certain she goes to bed with all those beautiful young people she brings home. This is not true; she should be trusted more. For even in the giving of her affection she weighs everything before committing. Her many friends are all beautiful people. Her serene disposition inclines her more toward romance than toward sexuality. Her room contains reproductions of old masters, and she insists that the family eat by candlelight and dress for dinner at least once a week so she can show off her emerald necklace and rings.

Leo: the second son has always been protected by Ari and Libby; consequently he has had more freedom. His red hair is sun-bleached, for he loves to surf. He is athletic, but not in a sweaty way; he is always drying off in the sun and cultivating his golden tan. In winter he is the leading man of the local little theater club; he loves the spotlight. His specialty in the stockbroker's office where he works is gambling on commodities futures. He is perennially broke; for he likes to buy nice things and is generous to a fault. He drives his father completely crazy with his spendthrift ways; and his mother tut-tuts after him as she picks up his new clothes from the bedroom floor, from the couch, from wherever else he drops them.

Aquarius: the second daughter — is slender. Her blond hair is a little unkempt; her glasses tend to hide her unusual violet eyes. She walks a little stooped as if the weight of the world's worries were on her shoulders. After a blowup with her "square" father, she left home and now has an apartment near her job as secretary to an association for the translation of philosophical works into African languages. In the last few years she has been accepted back into the family circle, though even now she sometimes rubs her father the wrong way with her irreverent remarks. She tends to wear sensible violet shawls that match her eyes and make her look older than her age. She is often vague and tends to lose the thread of the conversation.

Taurus: the third son — Torrie — is the dark one who takes after his father. Even though he has just left college, he has many expensive suits and wears a heavy gold chain on his wrist and another around his neck. His room (for he still lives at home) is over-full of good heavy furniture. He is energetic in his enterprises, which are always profit-oriented. He has some difficulty in selecting assistants; his greatest success has come from direct sales of luxury items to the rich. His only problem has been that he sometimes buys some of the things he is supposed to be selling. In fact, on one occasion it was suggested that he had borrowed something for his own use. He is often seen with a decorative older woman whom his mother hopes he sleeps with because she is concerned lest he be so miserly that he will never marry. Mother feels the older woman will take him off the shelf.

Pisces: the third daughter. In this, her final year at cosmetology school, Pisces has not changed her flaky behavior. She almost fails every course, but somehow her intelligence is pulling her through. She likes mod fashions, especially when they are layered, and she always buys pale lavender see-through garments that are too big for her. She boasts she has never owned a bra. She is slight and colorless, yet occasionally—when cornered—she can be very active. Because she drifts with the crowd, she has what used to be called round heels, for she falls into bed wherever she happens to be instead of bothering to go home. She has been arrested on minor charges, though there has never been sufficient evidence for a conviction. Because of these arrests, she worries that she is being watched; and to avoid being followed she sometimes goes to the police station and volunteers information. Father has completely given up on this one. His hopes that everything will turn out all right will be realized, for she will come to no harm.

Sagittarius: the youngest son—good old Saggi, with red hair and freckled face, puppy-like in his indiscriminate affection. When you meet him, Huck Finn immediately comes to mind. He is perennially cheerful and compulsively affectionate. He will attempt anything, for nothing daunts him. When he gets into trouble, he will tell the honest truth even if it means punishment; for he knows that his father will forgive him anything and his mother indulges him more than she does all the other children. Even Aunt Virgo smiles when he comes into the room and feeds him tidbits from her carefully arranged table. He can be found rolling around on the hearth-rug with his big English sheepdog. So numerous are his young friends that no one in the house, not even Uncle Scorpio, can keep track of them. They are always playing boisterously together, and Mother has to hush them constantly when Father is sleeping.

The Gemini Twins: last but not least are these young blond twins. They are just leaving high school. It is a good thing they have light responsibilities, because they are deplorably unreliable. They jump from one subject to another; their energy is fantastic, their span of attention zero. They are never seen in the same clothes twice, and are fond of trashy jewelry that clatters and glitters. If you tell one of them to meet you somewhere, you are never quite sure you told the right one — or that anyone was listening through the chatter anyway. These two are the lightest and brightest of the whole family. When they enter a room, it automatically starts to crackle. They frustrate the rest of the family, because one is sure to grab the TV remote control and flick around the channels. Even when she has found a program she likes and everyone is finally settled watching it and finished grumbling about the one they wanted to finish — she changes channels again.

.   .   .

Of course these are caricatures; but you will know many people who fit one part (if not all) of each archetype. Think of TV characters or characters from books you have read. If you can clearly visualize these images in your mind you will have more knowledge of human nature and more ability to predict.

Two Dials That Will Help

Now let's consider using these family members (or archetypes) in prediction. What will happen if Father Capricorn decides to wed a woman like his eldest daughter Libra? Obviously disaster will result, for he honestly has no understanding of her or of her ways. Nor can she comprehend him.

What if the roles are reversed and the reader is confronted with a female Capricorn and a male Libra? The father characteristics will tend to be accentuated in the female Capricorn mainly because in this day and age businesswomen are taking themselves far more seriously than they did years ago in their attempts to establish their identity and equality. The male Libra will have all the eldest daughter's characteristics — plus a tendency to wonder about his sexual preference; for he has been taught today that men are well advised to suppress their blatant macho behavior, and he has succeeded in doing so. You can immediately see how these two people could never get along. Advice of "travel further" would be beneficial here.

From such considerations comes the understanding that people who are separated by three months on the calendar are unable to work well together. Traditionally these relationships are called squares and figure 20 on page 102 is your instant aid in seeing which signs are square to one another.

Cut out the top circle and pin it to the center of the lower dial. (Actually we will repeat these figures at the end of the book to make this easier.) When you place Point A over the sign of one of the people involved, the arrows indicate the other family members who are incompatible with the one in question, and thus should be avoided in joint ventures and in marriage.

In a similar manner, when you look at the family, you know that Mother Cancer loves her third daughter Pisces who is always in trouble more than she does the other girls. And you know that although Mother has a good relationship with Papa Capricorn, she has a secret curiosity for his brother, the mysterious Scorpio who loves her in return and who has been to bed with daughter Pisces. Or rather — she went to sleep in his bed because it was the handiest one.

Uncle Scorpio and third son Taurus often go out together to enjoy a good meal. These close family relationships are shown in our astromantic friendship dial. You can construct the dial by pinning the upper disk of figure 21

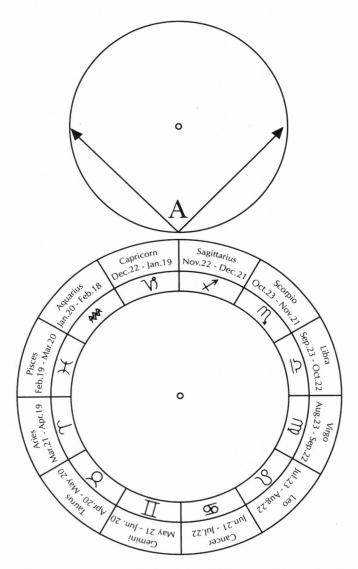

Figure 20.   Your astromantic incompatibility dial. Cut out the dial at the top of the figure. Pin it to the center of the bottom figure. Place Point A on your birthdate. Arrows will indicate incompatibilities. Or, you can use the duplicate figure at the end of the book.

(page 104) to the center of the lower dial. In traditional terms, these relationships are called trines, or the attraction of opposites.

One special relationship has grown up in the family. Many years ago when Ari was in trouble but did not dare tell Papa about it, Uncle Scorpio managed to come up with a scheme that saved the boy's bacon. Ever since, there has been a strong mutual bond. These two have been known to cruise together, more like brothers than like uncle and nephew.

If you look at the friendship computer dial, you can see the many interpersonal relationships in the family and can understand them. Father Capricorn and Aunt Virgo have a quiet friendship going. Maybe he sees in her some resemblance to his wife before she got so plump. Aunt Virgo loves Torrie, for she greatly approves his accumulation of wealth. She is not so sure about gold — but those green dollars. And she wouldn't for a moment believe that he sleeps with any of the women she sees him with. The aunt has a grudging admiration for daughter Pisces, too (perhaps she wishes she were more like her) and lives vicariously through Pisces' adventures.

Predictions about Ventures and Marriages

Businesses and marriages have natures of their own. A business or a marriage may often be internally inconsistent if it was started at an inappropriate time. Recent studies of biorhythms convince us that the use of the moon cycle of 28-$\frac{1}{2}$ days gives students a better feel for the future than does the older method used in traditional circles. That method (called progressions) arbitrarily equated a day with a year; only a few very highly qualified astrologers can handle it successfully. The elements of any venture will return at yearly intervals, but as the moon rotates, so will fortunes wax and wane. When selecting the best date for the start of a venture, first identify a date appropriate to the nature of the business or the marriage, or a compatible date; then within that

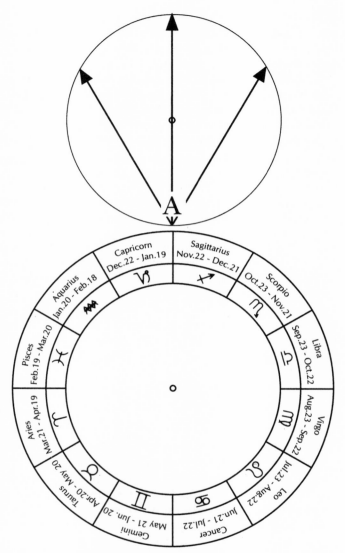

Figure 21. Your astromantic friendship dial. Cut out the dial at the top of the figure. Pin to the center of the bottom figure. Place Point A on your birthdate. Compatible friends and lovers will be found at the head of solid arrows. You can also use the duplicate figure found at the end of the book.

monthly span select a date immediately after the new moon. The venture will then grow with the growth of the moon and will suffer decline and growth in a cyclical way with the moon's phases. If you move the disk indicating the business around a wheel of fortune (figure 22) you will be able to see quite clearly which declines will be disastrous and which of the expansions will be most advantageous in the long haul. The art of managing the business will lie in seeing that there are reserves sufficient to weather the disastrous periods and that a full, firm push is given to the business just before a

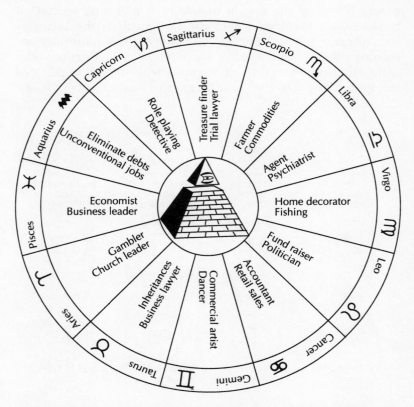

Figure 22. Businesses compatible with family members. Note: Color segments the same as disks in figure 23.

rise in its future so that the upswings are as large and as sustained as possible.

To Predict for Business Ventures

The businesses that best fit each of the family members are shown in figure 22. Use this figure in conjunction with your compatibility indicator to see that every business has the most chance of success when it is started in its basic sign dates (Table 7 on page 95) or in a trine with one of those dates. If one of the family members is planning to start a business, an auspicious date can be found. If the business has already been founded, its internal compatibility or incompatibility can readily be determined. Further, the compatibility of the type of business with the personality of the founder or founders can be gauged. Thus just by using

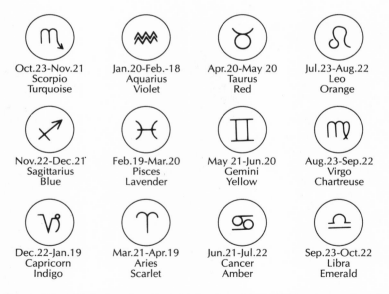

Oct.23-Nov.21 Scorpio Turquoise	Jan.20-Feb.-18 Aquarius Violet	Apr.20-May 20 Taurus Red	Jul.23-Aug.22 Leo Orange
Nov.22-Dec.21 Sagittarius Blue	Feb.19-Mar.20 Pisces Lavender	May 21-Jun.20 Gemini Yellow	Aug.23-Sep.22 Virgo Chartreuse
Dec.22-Jan.19 Capricorn Indigo	Mar.21-Apr.19 Aries Scarlet	Jun.21-Jul.22 Cancer Amber	Sep.23-Oct.22 Libra Emerald

Figure 23.   Disks for situation evaluation. Note: Make three of each type of disk.

the signs you can see how complicated is the problem that we have now set for ourselves.

So that you can visualize all this and contemplate it while your CC works, you should construct an astromantic fortune-telling wheel. Copy figure 22 (see page 105) onto a large piece of cardboard. Color it as indicated in the figure, but do not show the businesses indicated. Then make up a series of small disks (as shown in fig. 23). It is good to make three of each of the disks. Color these as indicated in the figure. Now place them at the appropriate position on the fortune-telling wheel.

Sit quietly and think about how the family members react with their backgrounds. An immediate feel can be gotten for the situation if you simply consider whether the colors clash or harmonize. Are all the disks grouped together in one or two segments? If so, the business will never show great worldly success and never diversify much, but will hum along harmoniously. Are the disks scattered in a random way? If so, the venture will be so diverse that it will never amount to much. Are the disks nicely balanced in sectors that make a triangle? This is the best possible arrangement, for in it you find stable growth.

You may find that if you move one of the disks either closer to the center or further from it, a better balanced position can be obtained. This means that the person represented by that disk should have more or less influence on the business. When close to the center, the person should be allowed more say in the decisions made; when at the outside edge, he or she should be involved only peripherally.

Obviously the placement of your disks on the fortune-telling wheel is critical. The first disk you place represents the business by its type. The second represents the inception date of the business; again place it within its appropriate segment. Subsequent disks represent the business partners. These are placed in the segment appropriate to their natal date. A small cardboard square and a triangle may help you decide on compatibilities and incompatibilities within the wheel of fortune.

Table 8. Illness or weakness
in body parts for family members.

Family Member	Illness	Body Part
MOTHER (Cancer)	Bronchitis Digestion Circulation	Breast Stomach
FATHER (Capricorn)	Glaucoma Palsy	Knees Bones Skin
UNCLE (Scorpio)	Impotence Muscle Tension	Pelvis Genitalia
AUNT (Virgo)	Cerebral Palsy Retardation	Hands Abdomen Intestines
ELDEST SON (Aries)	Arthritis Blood Pressure Depression Exhaustion	Head
ELDEST DAUGHTER (Libra)	Fever Hypertension Blood Disease	Lower Back Kidneys
SECOND SON (Leo)	Mononucleosis Cramps Thyroid	Heart Spine Arms Wrists
SECOND DAUGHTER (Aquarius)	Ulcer Epilepsy Diarrhea	Ankles
THIRD SON (Taurus)	Polio Melancholy Tuberculosis	Neck
THIRD DAUGHTER (Pisces)	Insomnia Tumor Irritation Herpes	Feet
YOUNGEST SON (Sagittarius)	Shingles Goiter	Hips Thighs Liver
YOUNGEST DAUGHTERS (Gemini)	Constipation Hepatitis, Diabetes	Hands Arms Lungs

If you are a competent astrologer, you can take three or four natal charts, transfer them to transparent material, and superimpose them on one another. Then placing them over a light box, you can immediately see the millions of interactions that will occur. For those of us who are less skilled, the Wheel of Fortune gives us a chance to use our Consciousness Connection to predict the outcome of partnerships and most of the problems that are brought to the reader. This work can be done in any way you like or feel is suitable. Health problems can also be analyzed by using the health-to-family-member correspondences shown in Table 8.

In your readings, always remember to consider how the family members will react and what the effect will be on the rest of the family when two or more of them make a partnership.

At first sight this method of using astrology may impress you as light-hearted and irresponsible, but you will find that as you grow accustomed to it, it will tell you more than you can use — and with greater accuracy — than many traditionally calculated charts, all their accurate mathematics notwithstanding.

Chapter 7

The I Ching

The *I Ching* is undoubtedly the oldest known predictive system whose history can be traced with any confidence. It is said that the gods gave us the *I Ching* and the junk-rigged sailing vessel to help us on this earth. In another Chinese myth, four old men representing the elements were the authors of the *Book of Changes*.

Originally the hexagrams of the *I Ching* were written as dots, circles, and crosses; the legendary King Wen (2205–1766 B.C.E.)[1] changed these to the linear representations we know today. At that time the hexagrams were used only to indicate changes and the future. It was King Wen's son, the Duke of Chou (who legend says died in 1150 B.C.E.) who wrote the *Book of Wisdom* that is now included in the *Book of Changes*. Legend also attributes to Confucius (Kung Fu Tse) a correction of some of Chou's work.

Many students of the *I Ching* regard every word both in the *Book of Changes* and in the *Book of Wisdom* with the same reverence a Christian fanatic feels toward Jehovah's words in the Bible. Remember, when you are using the *I Ching*, that its words were written in a distant land in a far-off time. In modern situations of which the original writers could have no knowledge, it is quite permissible to adapt or re-word the wisdom. Some philosophers go so far as to say that even in his 600-year life Duke Chou had many off days, and that it is

---

[1] Before Common Era.

permissible completely to re-interpret many hexagrams. All we say is: do not use too tight an interpretation, and always go back to the meaning of the original lines and the parts of the hexagram when you are in doubt.[2]

The Lines

The hexagram is a series of six lines spaced vertically one above the other. Two methods of casting the hexagrams are described on page 135. Both methods can result in four different types of line. They may be either broken or unbroken; examples are illustrated in figure 24. The solid (unbroken) lines are yang (male, thrusting, and aggressive), the broken lines are yin (female, passive, and receptive). Today many women feel that the attributes of passivity and receptivity are a chauvinist male's way of putting them down; the Chinese response to this is the changing line. As shown in figure 24(c) a yin line with a cross in its center becomes a yang line which is called *old yin*. This says that as a woman matures, she grows from passivity and receptivity, and takes on more assertive yang attributes.

In a similar way, the line in figure 24(b) is though to be *old yang*, where in age yang takes on some of the passivity and receptivity of the yin. Changing lines are traditionally drawn as shown in fig. 24(a): a broken line with a cross for old yin and a broken line with a circle for old yang. By

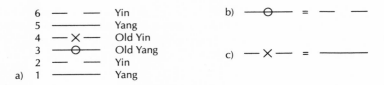

Figure 24. The lines of the hexagram.

[2]We recommend the Richard Wilhelm translation. *Lectures on the I Ching* (Princeton University Press, 1986; and London: Routledge, 1968).

common usage, then, the plain unbroken line becomes *young yang* and the plain broken line becomes *young yin*, as shown in the figure.

During a reading the hexagram is read first without changing the lines. As a situation is considered to develop, then the lines are changed to show that development. This will be discussed further in reference to figure 27 on page 117.

The Trigrams

The trigrams are the most important aid to the reading, for they allow the reader to break any problem down into its basic (present) and future parts. Figure 25 shows a typical hexagram broken into its two component trigrams. The hexagram is always written and read from the bottom upward, for all things grow upward. The lines are said to be "in places" Number 1 at the bottom and Number 6 at the top. Trigram 1 is the lower, and trigram 2 is the upper. Each consists of three lines. The lower trigram is the basis for the problem; it can be associated with sickness in anything below the breast; or with activities related to the soil: mining, agriculture, fishing, and so on. The upper trigram (2) indicates matters relevant to sickness above the breast, and covers nervous diseases and moral questions. It can also be construed as the future and the gathering of wealth above the ground, like the harvesting of grain or the rents from houses and apartments.

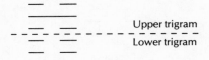

Figure 25. The trigrams.

The Meanings of the Trigrams

Whereas there are 64 basic hexagrams, there are only eight basic trigrams. You must thoroughly memorize the meanings of the trigrams. With that knowledge firmly in your mind, the meaning of the hexagram becomes vastly easier both to understand and to derive in the midst of a reading. Flipping pages to look something up is unnerving to the subject.

The trigrams can be thought of as going in a circle, moving from age and aggression through youth back to age and passivity; from triple-yang with its highly aggressive characteristics through youth to triple-yin with its total passivity. See figure 26.

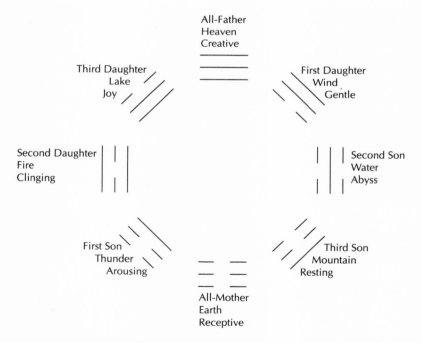

Figure 26.   The circle of trigrams.

In our study and use of the *I Ching*, we have found that the ancient family relationship metaphor gives the most meaningful modern results, and the avoidance of unfamiliar Chinese vocabulary is beneficial.

The Father: The one, creative, strong, and dynamic. The skies above in the middle of a storm, or the bright hot sun.

The First Son: Just after puberty his instincts are being aroused. Foolish aggression. Lots of movement. The thunder in the clouds, still hidden behind his father's clouds and lightning, but about to move out.

The Second Son: This is the son at puberty and dangerous. His balance can be disturbed at any time. His thoughts cannot be understood by those around him. He can be thought of as rough water, beating itself on a beach. Most of the time, his dangerous energy dissipates itself; but occasionally his forces gather, especially if his father or one of his sisters helps. He is particularly unstable when his elder sister is in trouble, and is likely to become uncontrollable in her defense.

The Third Son: This is the new-born son. He tends to keep quiet, especially in the presence of his elders. The forces here are under the control of his mother. He still "bides," as the saying goes, knowing that he is not yet strong enough to fight as his elder brothers do.

The All-Mother: Mother Nature. Totally receptive and passive, accepting all the things her children and her husband, the Father, do to her. She is symbolized by the good black earth. She is solid, altogether reliable. Wealth comes to her through the earth.

The First Daughter: This is the daughter after being married or having had several lovers. She is gentle, but her emotions are easily roused. Even when this happens, she is still not aggressive. Often this stage is not reached by Western women until after their children have left; but with the different Chinese sexual mores, it was assumed that women achieved this stage in their early 20's. She is represented as the gentle wind often blowing through a woodland scene and bending the trees. Only when she is endangered does the wind become cold and penetrating and powerful.

The Second Daughter: She is embarking on her first tentative love affair. She is clinging, and her aura of happiness gives light to everyone around her. Her love consumes everything in its path; thus she can be thought of as "fire."

The Third Daughter: She is a young happy girl who gives joy and happiness wherever she goes. She is the placid lake with boats around its side, standing ready for life's journey. She does not represent the aggressive movement of the male youths, for when you go with the third daughter on a journey, you will return to the place you left; but you know that the journey will be full of light and joyful, for nothing heavy can be a part of her makeup.

Changing Lines

In the mechanics of casting the hexagram, some lines can come out that are called *changing*; others are *fixed*. As the hexagram is constructed, the changing lines are read as yin and yang; then a second hexagram is constructed with the lines changed. The operation is shown in figure 27 (page 117). The hexagram in fig. 27a is read first as shown in fig. 27b, then it is read as in fig. 27c. The first reading is considered the present situation (the Well), and the second one is the future (Grace).

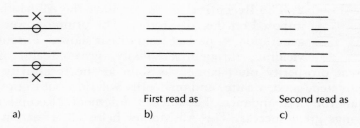

a)   First read as   Second read as
                             b)   c)

Figure 27.   The effect of changing lines.

Because of the complexity of the readings for individual line changes, we leave these to the more advanced reader. We recommend that for now you read only the original hexagram and the changed hexagram, and that you restrict your readings of line changes to the obvious effect of, say, changing from weaker to stronger or vice versa.

The Hexagrams

Below is a list of 64 hexagrams and their interpretations. Table 9 (page 134) is the key to finding the hexagrams from the trigrams. Identifying the lower trigram first and then going across the Table and finding the upper trigram will give the number of the hexagrams far more quickly than will trying to go through all 64 hexagrams looking for the one that matches the one you have cast.

1. The Creative: This is the ultimate force. It may be regarded as God in Its creative aspect. It is total strength, power, and energy; it is also all Time. Thus the energy of the creation will not be lost even though Time flows, for the energy persists. It is more the creation of the Sage than of the Builder. When this hexagram appears, creative writing will succeed. It is the charismatic leader with the positive, creative message. The ancient judgment: "The Creative works sublime success, benefiting all through perseverance."

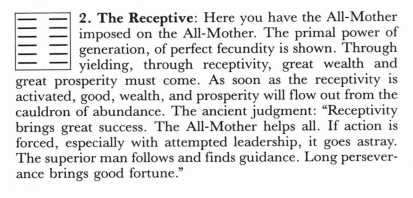 **2. The Receptive**: Here you have the All-Mother imposed on the All-Mother. The primal power of generation, of perfect fecundity is shown. Through yielding, through receptivity, great wealth and great prosperity must come. As soon as the receptivity is activated, good, wealth, and prosperity will flow out from the cauldron of abundance. The ancient judgment: "Receptivity brings great success. The All-Mother helps all. If action is forced, especially with attempted leadership, it goes astray. The superior man follows and finds guidance. Long perseverance brings good fortune."

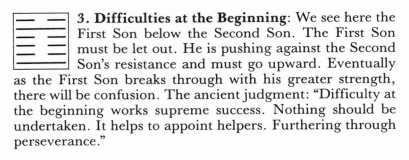 **3. Difficulties at the Beginning**: We see here the First Son below the Second Son. The First Son must be let out. He is pushing against the Second Son's resistance and must go upward. Eventually as the First Son breaks through with his greater strength, there will be confusion. The ancient judgment: "Difficulty at the beginning works supreme success. Nothing should be undertaken. It helps to appoint helpers. Furthering through perseverance."

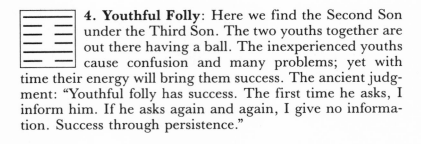 **4. Youthful Folly**: Here we find the Second Son under the Third Son. The two youths together are out there having a ball. The inexperienced youths cause confusion and many problems; yet with time their energy will bring them success. The ancient judgment: "Youthful folly has success. The first time he asks, I inform him. If he asks again and again, I give no information. Success through persistence."

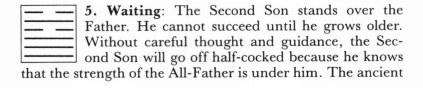 **5. Waiting**: The Second Son stands over the Father. He cannot succeed until he grows older. Without careful thought and guidance, the Second Son will go off half-cocked because he knows that the strength of the All-Father is under him. The ancient

judgment: "Waiting. If you are sincere, you will have light and success. Persistence brings good fortune. Travel is a benefit."

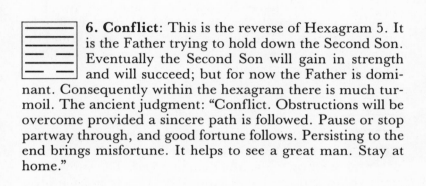 **6. Conflict**: This is the reverse of Hexagram 5. It is the Father trying to hold down the Second Son. Eventually the Second Son will gain in strength and will succeed; but for now the Father is dominant. Consequently within the hexagram there is much turmoil. The ancient judgment: "Conflict. Obstructions will be overcome provided a sincere path is followed. Pause or stop partway through, and good fortune follows. Persisting to the end brings misfortune. It helps to see a great man. Stay at home."

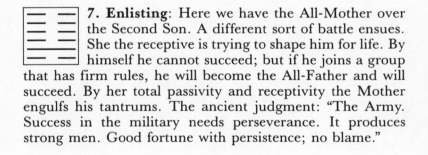 **7. Enlisting**: Here we have the All-Mother over the Second Son. A different sort of battle ensues. She the receptive is trying to shape him for life. By himself he cannot succeed; but if he joins a group that has firm rules, he will become the All-Father and will succeed. By her total passivity and receptivity the Mother engulfs his tantrums. The ancient judgment: "The Army. Success in the military needs perseverance. It produces strong men. Good fortune with persistence; no blame."

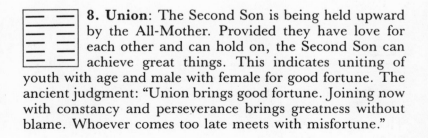 **8. Union**: The Second Son is being held upward by the All-Mother. Provided they have love for each other and can hold on, the Second Son can achieve great things. This indicates uniting of youth with age and male with female for good fortune. The ancient judgment: "Union brings good fortune. Joining now with constancy and perseverance brings greatness without blame. Whoever comes too late meets with misfortune."

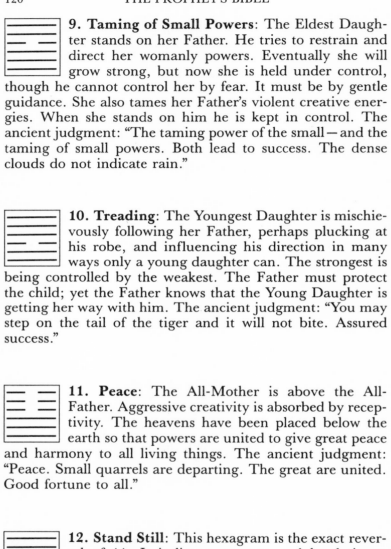

9. Taming of Small Powers: The Eldest Daughter stands on her Father. He tries to restrain and direct her womanly powers. Eventually she will grow strong, but now she is held under control, though he cannot control her by fear. It must be by gentle guidance. She also tames her Father's violent creative energies. When she stands on him he is kept in control. The ancient judgment: "The taming power of the small — and the taming of small powers. Both lead to success. The dense clouds do not indicate rain."

10. Treading: The Youngest Daughter is mischievously following her Father, perhaps plucking at his robe, and influencing his direction in many ways only a young daughter can. The strongest is being controlled by the weakest. The Father must protect the child; yet the Father knows that the Young Daughter is getting her way with him. The ancient judgment: "You may step on the tail of the tiger and it will not bite. Assured success."

11. Peace: The All-Mother is above the All-Father. Aggressive creativity is absorbed by receptivity. The heavens have been placed below the earth so that powers are united to give great peace and harmony to all living things. The ancient judgment: "Peace. Small quarrels are departing. The great are united. Good fortune to all."

12. Stand Still: This hexagram is the exact reversal of 11. It indicates poverty and hard times. Heaven dominates earth; the male dominates the female. This leads to divorce, confusion, and disorder. The ancient judgment: "Stand still. Nothing furthers. The superior man quietly perseveres. The great departs, the small approaches. Do not seek gain."

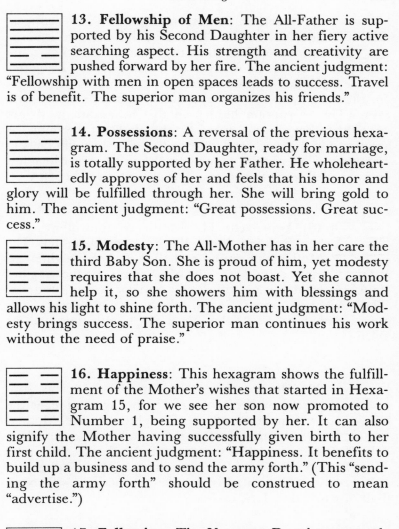

13. Fellowship of Men: The All-Father is supported by his Second Daughter in her fiery active searching aspect. His strength and creativity are pushed forward by her fire. The ancient judgment: "Fellowship with men in open spaces leads to success. Travel is of benefit. The superior man organizes his friends."

14. Possessions: A reversal of the previous hexagram. The Second Daughter, ready for marriage, is totally supported by her Father. He wholeheartedly approves of her and feels that his honor and glory will be fulfilled through her. She will bring gold to him. The ancient judgment: "Great possessions. Great success."

15. Modesty: The All-Mother has in her care the third Baby Son. She is proud of him, yet modesty requires that she does not boast. Yet she cannot help it, so she showers him with blessings and allows his light to shine forth. The ancient judgment: "Modesty brings success. The superior man continues his work without the need of praise."

16. Happiness: This hexagram shows the fulfillment of the Mother's wishes that started in Hexagram 15, for we see her son now promoted to Number 1, being supported by her. It can also signify the Mother having successfully given birth to her first child. The ancient judgment: "Happiness. It benefits to build up a business and to send the army forth." (This "sending the army forth" should be construed to mean "advertise.")

17. Following: The Youngest Daughter controls the First Son. With her joy and youthful energy she leads her older brother around by his nose. The strong young man runs after the pretty little girl and she twirls him around her little finger. The ancient judgment: "The follower is successful. It is of great benefit to continue to follow. No blame."

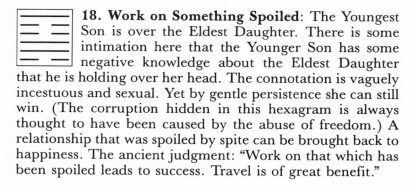

18. Work on Something Spoiled: The Youngest Son is over the Eldest Daughter. There is some intimation here that the Younger Son has some negative knowledge about the Eldest Daughter that he is holding over her head. The connotation is vaguely incestuous and sexual. Yet by gentle persistence she can still win. (The corruption hidden in this hexagram is always thought to have been caused by the abuse of freedom.) A relationship that was spoiled by spite can be brought back to happiness. The ancient judgment: "Work on that which has been spoiled leads to success. Travel is of great benefit."

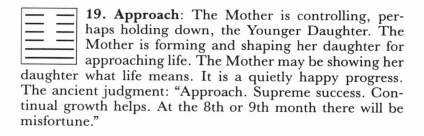

19. Approach: The Mother is controlling, perhaps holding down, the Younger Daughter. The Mother is forming and shaping her daughter for approaching life. The Mother may be showing her daughter what life means. It is a quietly happy progress. The ancient judgment: "Approach. Supreme success. Continual growth helps. At the 8th or 9th month there will be misfortune."

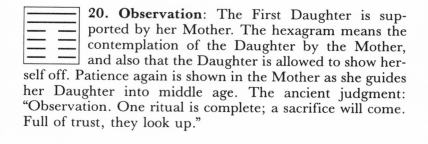

20. Observation: The First Daughter is supported by her Mother. The hexagram means the contemplation of the Daughter by the Mother, and also that the Daughter is allowed to show herself off. Patience again is shown in the Mother as she guides her Daughter into middle age. The ancient judgment: "Observation. One ritual is complete; a sacrifice will come. Full of trust, they look up."

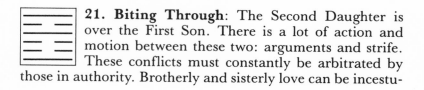

21. Biting Through: The Second Daughter is over the First Son. There is a lot of action and motion between these two: arguments and strife. These conflicts must constantly be arbitrated by those in authority. Brotherly and sisterly love can be incestuous. The rules must always be obeyed, and no shortcuts can be taken. The ancient judgment: "Biting through to the core of the problem leads to success. It is best to let justice be administered and follow the rules."

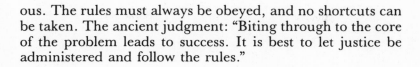 **22. Grace**: The Second Daughter carries the Youngest Son. Both are beautiful. With the litheness of youth she carries his resting body gracefully. The fire breaks through and illuminates his qualities. The ancient judgment: "Gracefulness will bring success. Small details of correction benefit. It is favorable to undertake something small."

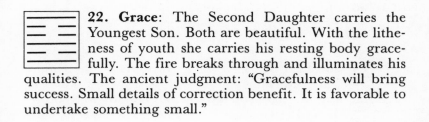 **23. Splitting Apart**: The Third Son is about to leave the Mother. All sons must eventually leave the Mother's influence. It is a time for caution and gentle moves; otherwise a violent quarrel will result, the Son will go on a journey, and the Mother will be distraught. The ancient judgment: "Splitting apart: it is unfavorable to undertake anything."

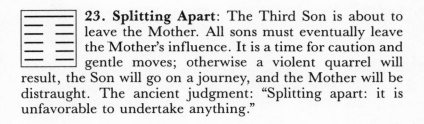 **24. Return**: The Eldest Son has returned to support the Mother. After being away he has come back. He now has greater understanding and greater appreciation of his Mother's qualities. The time of their separation is past and they now will grow together in ever-greater harmony. The ancient judgment: "Return brings success. One who has gone away comes back in without harm. Friends will come back without blame. To and fro goes the way. On the 7th day, return again. It benefits one to have places to go."

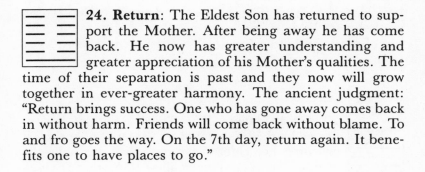 **25. The Unexpected**: The Father controls his Eldest Son. Again the Son has returned to support the Father; suddenly in a flash of understanding he realizes the strength and creativity of his father.

The realization can be a spiritual awakening, or a misfortune from without. There are no ulterior motives in his return. He is happy to be once again under the shadow of his Father. The ancient judgment: "The unexpected. Supreme success. Benefit accrues through perseverance. A deceptive man has misfortune. No benefit for undertakings."

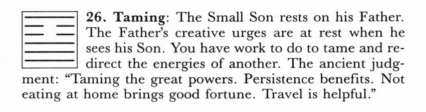

26. Taming: The Small Son rests on his Father. The Father's creative urges are at rest when he sees his Son. You have work to do to tame and redirect the energies of another. The ancient judgment: "Taming the great powers. Persistence benefits. Not eating at home brings good fortune. Travel is helpful."

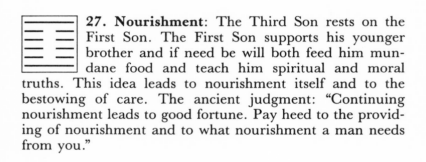

27. Nourishment: The Third Son rests on the First Son. The First Son supports his younger brother and if need be will both feed him mundane food and teach him spiritual and moral truths. This idea leads to nourishment itself and to the bestowing of care. The ancient judgment: "Continuing nourishment leads to good fortune. Pay heed to the providing of nourishment and to what nourishment a man needs from you."

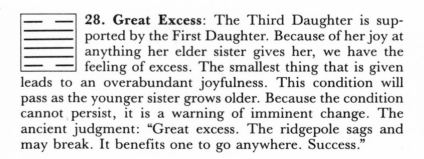

28. Great Excess: The Third Daughter is supported by the First Daughter. Because of her joy at anything her elder sister gives her, we have the feeling of excess. The smallest thing that is given leads to an overabundant joyfulness. This condition will pass as the younger sister grows older. Because the condition cannot persist, it is a warning of imminent change. The ancient judgment: "Great excess. The ridgepole sags and may break. It benefits one to go anywhere. Success."

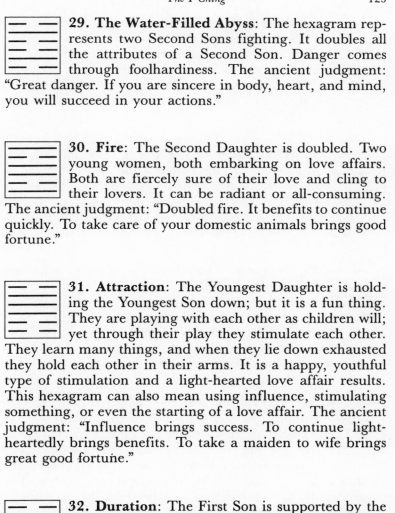

29. The Water-Filled Abyss: The hexagram represents two Second Sons fighting. It doubles all the attributes of a Second Son. Danger comes through foolhardiness. The ancient judgment: "Great danger. If you are sincere in body, heart, and mind, you will succeed in your actions."

30. Fire: The Second Daughter is doubled. Two young women, both embarking on love affairs. Both are fiercely sure of their love and cling to their lovers. It can be radiant or all-consuming. The ancient judgment: "Doubled fire. It benefits to continue quickly. To take care of your domestic animals brings good fortune."

31. Attraction: The Youngest Daughter is holding the Youngest Son down; but it is a fun thing. They are playing with each other as children will; yet through their play they stimulate each other. They learn many things, and when they lie down exhausted they hold each other in their arms. It is a happy, youthful type of stimulation and a light-hearted love affair results. This hexagram can also mean using influence, stimulating something, or even the starting of a love affair. The ancient judgment: "Influence brings success. To continue light-heartedly brings benefits. To take a maiden to wife brings great good fortune."

32. Duration: The First Son is supported by the First Daughter. They will always love one another and will be together forever. The Son is supported by the Daughter, and an enduring marriage results when the husband is supported by the wife. The ancient judgment: "Success occurs after a long time. No blame. Perseverance furthers. It furthers one to have somewhere to go."

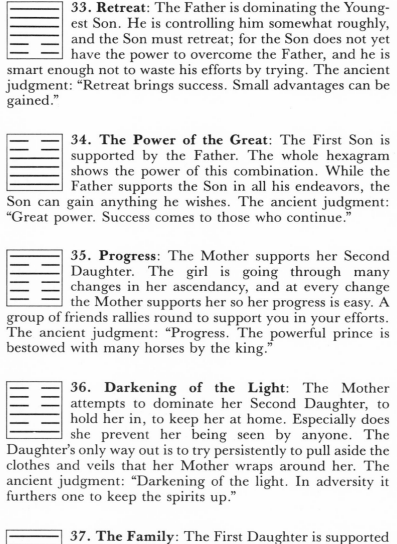

33. Retreat: The Father is dominating the Youngest Son. He is controlling him somewhat roughly, and the Son must retreat; for the Son does not yet have the power to overcome the Father, and he is smart enough not to waste his efforts by trying. The ancient judgment: "Retreat brings success. Small advantages can be gained."

34. The Power of the Great: The First Son is supported by the Father. The whole hexagram shows the power of this combination. While the Father supports the Son in all his endeavors, the Son can gain anything he wishes. The ancient judgment: "Great power. Success comes to those who continue."

35. Progress: The Mother supports her Second Daughter. The girl is going through many changes in her ascendancy, and at every change the Mother supports her so her progress is easy. A group of friends rallies round to support you in your efforts. The ancient judgment: "Progress. The powerful prince is bestowed with many horses by the king."

36. Darkening of the Light: The Mother attempts to dominate her Second Daughter, to hold her in, to keep her at home. Especially does she prevent her being seen by anyone. The Daughter's only way out is to try persistently to pull aside the clothes and veils that her Mother wraps around her. The ancient judgment: "Darkening of the light. In adversity it furthers one to keep the spirits up."

37. The Family: The First Daughter is supported by the Second Daughter; a strong friendship results. The power of the family is shown here when it is confronted with outside dangers. The ancient judgment: "The family. The perseverance of the family unit benefits all."

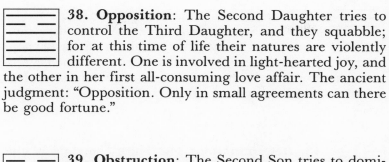 **38. Opposition**: The Second Daughter tries to control the Third Daughter, and they squabble; for at this time of life their natures are violently different. One is involved in light-hearted joy, and the other in her first all-consuming love affair. The ancient judgment: "Opposition. Only in small agreements can there be good fortune."

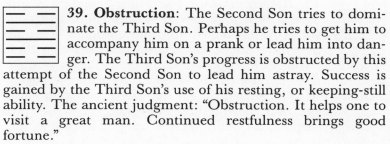 **39. Obstruction**: The Second Son tries to dominate the Third Son. Perhaps he tries to get him to accompany him on a prank or lead him into danger. The Third Son's progress is obstructed by this attempt of the Second Son to lead him astray. Success is gained by the Third Son's use of his resting, or keeping-still ability. The ancient judgment: "Obstruction. It helps one to visit a great man. Continued restfulness brings good fortune."

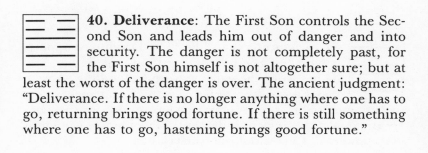 **40. Deliverance**: The First Son controls the Second Son and leads him out of danger and into security. The danger is not completely past, for the First Son himself is not altogether sure; but at least the worst of the danger is over. The ancient judgment: "Deliverance. If there is no longer anything where one has to go, returning brings good fortune. If there is still something where one has to go, hastening brings good fortune."

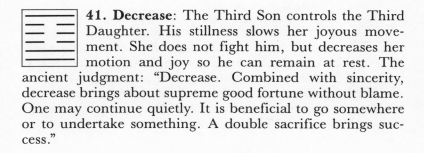 **41. Decrease**: The Third Son controls the Third Daughter. His stillness slows her joyous movement. She does not fight him, but decreases her motion and joy so he can remain at rest. The ancient judgment: "Decrease. Combined with sincerity, decrease brings about supreme good fortune without blame. One may continue quietly. It is beneficial to go somewhere or to undertake something. A double sacrifice brings success."

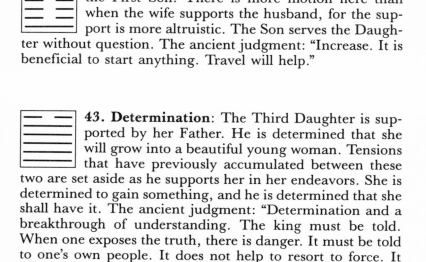

42. Increase: The First Daughter is supported by the First Son. There is more motion here than when the wife supports the husband, for the support is more altruistic. The Son serves the Daughter without question. The ancient judgment: "Increase. It is beneficial to start anything. Travel will help."

43. Determination: The Third Daughter is supported by her Father. He is determined that she will grow into a beautiful young woman. Tensions that have previously accumulated between these two are set aside as he supports her in her endeavors. She is determined to gain something, and he is determined that she shall have it. The ancient judgment: "Determination and a breakthrough of understanding. The king must be told. When one exposes the truth, there is danger. It must be told to one's own people. It does not help to resort to force. It furthers one to undertake something else."

44. Encountering: The First Daughter supports her Father. She fully understands her Father, and by her words he gains new understanding. A man meets a mature woman; a woman may meet many mature men. This is not a marriage hexagram, for the parts are unequal. The ancient judgment: "The mature woman is very powerful. One should not marry her."

45. Gathering: The Youngest Daughter is supported by her Mother. The Mother is holding her, listening, absorbing the multitude of her ideas. The young daughters gather around the Mother, merrily enjoying her placidity. The ancient judgment: "Gathering together leads to success. The king joins with his priests. It is helpful to see a great person. A great sacrifice leads to good fortune. It furthers one to undertake something or to go somewhere."

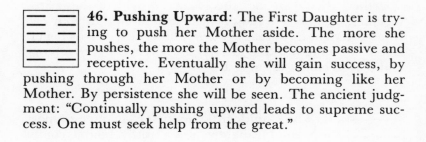 **46. Pushing Upward**: The First Daughter is trying to push her Mother aside. The more she pushes, the more the Mother becomes passive and receptive. Eventually she will gain success, by pushing through her Mother or by becoming like her Mother. By persistence she will be seen. The ancient judgment: "Continually pushing upward leads to supreme success. One must seek help from the great."

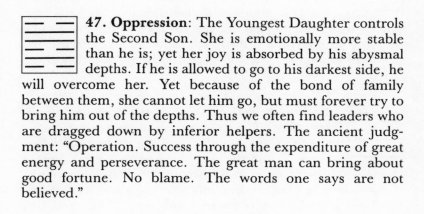 **47. Oppression**: The Youngest Daughter controls the Second Son. She is emotionally more stable than he is; yet her joy is absorbed by his abysmal depths. If he is allowed to go to his darkest side, he will overcome her. Yet because of the bond of family between them, she cannot let him go, but must forever try to bring him out of the depths. Thus we often find leaders who are dragged down by inferior helpers. The ancient judgment: "Operation. Success through the expenditure of great energy and perseverance. The great man can bring about good fortune. No blame. The words one says are not believed."

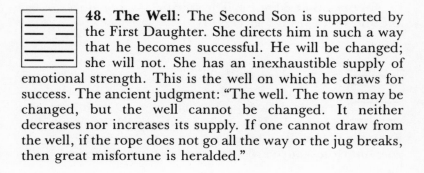 **48. The Well**: The Second Son is supported by the First Daughter. She directs him in such a way that he becomes successful. He will be changed; she will not. She has an inexhaustible supply of emotional strength. This is the well on which he draws for success. The ancient judgment: "The well. The town may be changed, but the well cannot be changed. It neither decreases nor increases its supply. If one cannot draw from the well, if the rope does not go all the way or the jug breaks, then great misfortune is heralded."

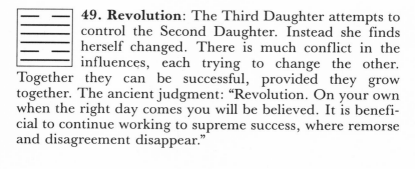 **49. Revolution**: The Third Daughter attempts to control the Second Daughter. Instead she finds herself changed. There is much conflict in the influences, each trying to change the other. Together they can be successful, provided they grow together. The ancient judgment: "Revolution. On your own when the right day comes you will be believed. It is beneficial to continue working to supreme success, where remorse and disagreement disappear."

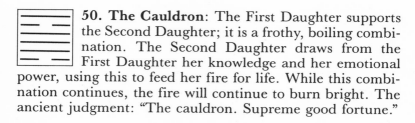 **50. The Cauldron**: The First Daughter supports the Second Daughter; it is a frothy, boiling combination. The Second Daughter draws from the First Daughter her knowledge and her emotional power, using this to feed her fire for life. While this combination continues, the fire will continue to burn bright. The ancient judgment: "The cauldron. Supreme good fortune."

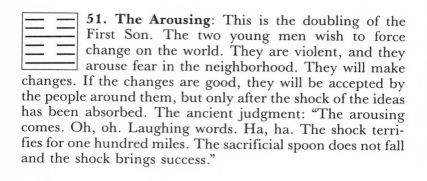 **51. The Arousing**: This is the doubling of the First Son. The two young men wish to force change on the world. They are violent, and they arouse fear in the neighborhood. They will make changes. If the changes are good, they will be accepted by the people around them, but only after the shock of the ideas has been absorbed. The ancient judgment: "The arousing comes. Oh, oh. Laughing words. Ha, ha. The shock terrifies for one hundred miles. The sacrificial spoon does not fall and the shock brings success."

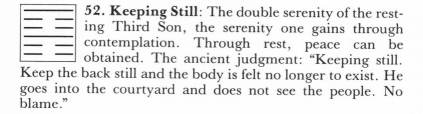 **52. Keeping Still**: The double serenity of the resting Third Son, the serenity one gains through contemplation. Through rest, peace can be obtained. The ancient judgment: "Keeping still. Keep the back still and the body is felt no longer to exist. He goes into the courtyard and does not see the people. No blame."

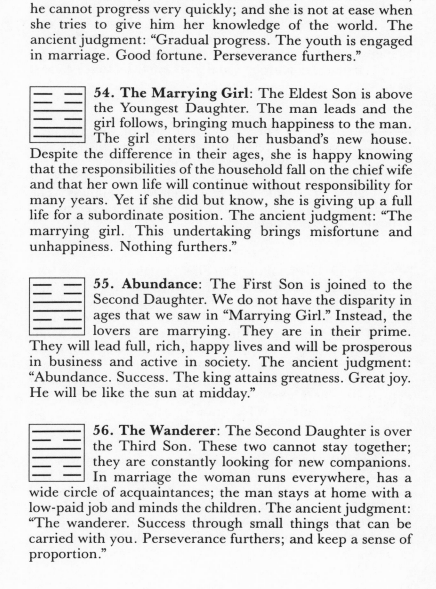

53. Gradual Progress: The First Daughter is relying on the Third Son. He is a firm, restful base; but from him she gains only a small amount of stability. Because she is so much older than he is, he cannot progress very quickly; and she is not at ease when she tries to give him her knowledge of the world. The ancient judgment: "Gradual progress. The youth is engaged in marriage. Good fortune. Perseverance furthers."

54. The Marrying Girl: The Eldest Son is above the Youngest Daughter. The man leads and the girl follows, bringing much happiness to the man. The girl enters into her husband's new house. Despite the difference in their ages, she is happy knowing that the responsibilities of the household fall on the chief wife and that her own life will continue without responsibility for many years. Yet if she did but know, she is giving up a full life for a subordinate position. The ancient judgment: "The marrying girl. This undertaking brings misfortune and unhappiness. Nothing furthers."

55. Abundance: The First Son is joined to the Second Daughter. We do not have the disparity in ages that we saw in "Marrying Girl." Instead, the lovers are marrying. They are in their prime. They will lead full, rich, happy lives and will be prosperous in business and active in society. The ancient judgment: "Abundance. Success. The king attains greatness. Great joy. He will be like the sun at midday."

56. The Wanderer: The Second Daughter is over the Third Son. These two cannot stay together; they are constantly looking for new companions. In marriage the woman runs everywhere, has a wide circle of acquaintances; the man stays at home with a low-paid job and minds the children. The ancient judgment: "The wanderer. Success through small things that can be carried with you. Perseverance furthers; and keep a sense of proportion."

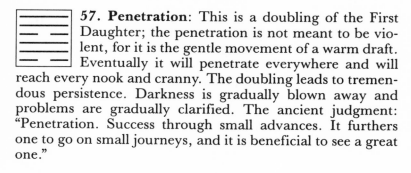 **57. Penetration**: This is a doubling of the First Daughter; the penetration is not meant to be violent, for it is the gentle movement of a warm draft. Eventually it will penetrate everywhere and will reach every nook and cranny. The doubling leads to tremendous persistence. Darkness is gradually blown away and problems are gradually clarified. The ancient judgment: "Penetration. Success through small advances. It furthers one to go on small journeys, and it is beneficial to see a great one."

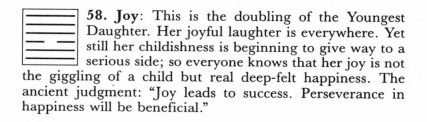 **58. Joy**: This is the doubling of the Youngest Daughter. Her joyful laughter is everywhere. Yet still her childishness is beginning to give way to a serious side; so everyone knows that her joy is not the giggling of a child but real deep-felt happiness. The ancient judgment: "Joy leads to success. Perseverance in happiness will be beneficial."

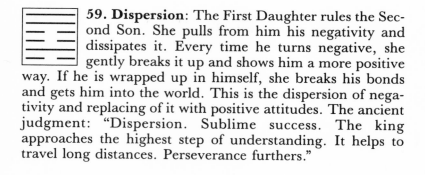 **59. Dispersion**: The First Daughter rules the Second Son. She pulls from him his negativity and dissipates it. Every time he turns negative, she gently breaks it up and shows him a more positive way. If he is wrapped up in himself, she breaks his bonds and gets him into the world. This is the dispersion of negativity and replacing of it with positive attitudes. The ancient judgment: "Dispersion. Sublime success. The king approaches the highest step of understanding. It helps to travel long distances. Perseverance furthers."

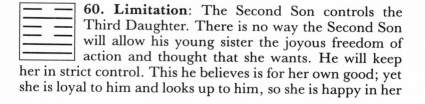 **60. Limitation**: The Second Son controls the Third Daughter. There is no way the Second Son will allow his young sister the joyous freedom of action and thought that she wants. He will keep her in strict control. This he believes is for her own good; yet she is loyal to him and looks up to him, so she is happy in her

more limited existence. The ancient judgment: "Limitation. Success. The limitations should not be continued; otherwise misfortune."

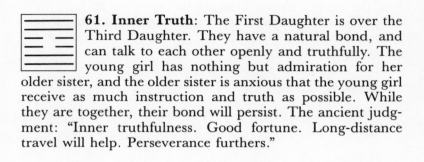 **61. Inner Truth**: The First Daughter is over the Third Daughter. They have a natural bond, and can talk to each other openly and truthfully. The young girl has nothing but admiration for her older sister, and the older sister is anxious that the young girl receive as much instruction and truth as possible. While they are together, their bond will persist. The ancient judgment: "Inner truthfulness. Good fortune. Long-distance travel will help. Perseverance furthers."

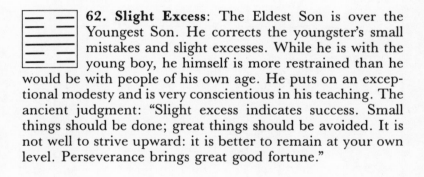 **62. Slight Excess**: The Eldest Son is over the Youngest Son. He corrects the youngster's small mistakes and slight excesses. While he is with the young boy, he himself is more restrained than he would be with people of his own age. He puts on an exceptional modesty and is very conscientious in his teaching. The ancient judgment: "Slight excess indicates success. Small things should be done; great things should be avoided. It is not well to strive upward: it is better to remain at your own level. Perseverance brings great good fortune."

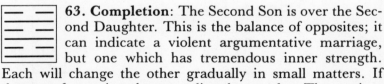 **63. Completion**: The Second Son is over the Second Daughter. This is the balance of opposites; it can indicate a violent argumentative marriage, but one which has tremendous inner strength. Each will change the other gradually in small matters. If they try for major changes, disorder results. The ancient judgment: "Completion. Success one step at a time. At the beginning good fortune. It benefits to continue small steps; otherwise disorder at the end."

64. Before Completion: This is the reverse of Hexagram 63, Completion. The transition from disorder to order is not yet complete, and will be violent. There is a hopeful part of this hexagram: it has a parallel to spring that leads out of the frozen winter into the bright loving flame of spring. The ancient judgment: "Success comes before completion; but if the little fox, after nearly completing the crossing, gets his tail in the water, nothing furthers."

Table 9. Finding the hexagrams from the trigrams.

Upper Trigrams → Lower Trigrams ↓								
	1	34	5	26	11	9	14	43
	25	51	3	27	24	42	21	17
	6	40	29	4	7	59	64	47
	33	62	39	52	15	53	56	31
	12	16	8	23	2	20	35	45
	44	32	48	18	46	57	50	28
	13	55	63	22	36	37	30	49
	10	54	60	41	19	61	38	58

Casting the Hexagram

Ancient Method: Formerly 24 yarrow stalks used to be used. Actually 24 smooth round stalks of any sort will do very well — quarter-inch doweling cut up into nine inch lengths, bamboo stalks, or even the stems of long fireplace matches are fine. Leave six stalks plain; paint six in the center with white or silver paint; give another six a black band; and give the last six a red band. Keep the 24 stalks stored in a tubular holder that contains them loosely.

To mix or shuffle the stalks before a reading, roll their ends with your hands. Select four at random and place them in the interstices of the fingers and thumb of one hand whose palm is upward. Gently toss the stalks into the air and quickly withdraw your hand, letting them fall on a silk cloth. The stalk that falls uppermost tells what the line will be. A plain stalk is an unbroken yang; a stalk with a black band is the broken yin; a stalk with a white band is the changing old yang; a stalk with a red band is the changing old yin.

If no stalk falls clearly uppermost, repeat the process with the same set of stalks. If one does fall uppermost, it is placed in the first position of the hexagram and the other five stalks go back into the set, where you again mix them and repeat the process until a total of six lines is defined. This is an elegant, pleasant way to cast the hexagram; it is one in which there can be conversation between the reader and the subject so the CC can come into play.

Modern Method: Currently the convention is to use three coins. Ideally these will be Chinese coins with a square hole in the center. The side with four Chinese characters is given a value of 3; the side with two Chinese characters is given a value of 2. If occidental coins are used, the heads side is given a value of 3 and the tails side equals 2 (Exception: when the coin bears the head of a woman, the head is given a value of 2 and the tails a 3.) Put the three coins gently into a wooden cup and shake them gently. Cast them onto a silk cloth. The sum of the numbers shown gives the line value. 6 is the changing old yin; 7 is the unchanging yang; 8 is the unchanging yin; 9 is the changing old yang.

The casting of the hexagrams is a way of communicating with Greater Wisdom; as such it should be approached in a spirit of deep respect, and much attention to detail is appropriate. The reader should be attired in a long flowing robe of silk or silk-like fabric, ideally colored red and black.[3] The coins and their cup (or the stalks in their tube) should be stored in an exotically carved box, wrapped in black silk. The more sincerity and reverence you bring to the casting, the more likely will be your success. A habit of taking just any old three coins and flinging them down should be avoided.

If you memorize fig. 24, remember to read the unchanged hexagram first and the changed hexagram second. You will have great success and good fortune with the *I Ching*. Perseverance furthers!

---

[3]In Chinese symbolism, black represents life and red represents happiness.

Chapter 8

The Tarot

The tarot is often all things to all people; each card contains symbols that can be interpreted on an astrological level, from its color and pattern, numerologically, historically. When they work with black and white Rohrschach cards, psychologists are using just one small part of a very poor tarot deck, for they are using a monochrome pattern-recognition system. Many psychologists we know have discarded the Rohrschach cards almost entirely in favor of tarot cards, for they can get far more from their patients by use of the rich tarot symbology than from cold inkblots.

The tarot card reader serves as a psychologist; the subject has a problem that needs to be solved. When the reader asks the subject, "What do you see in the card?" he or she can talk about the pictures in the card instead of the problem; this de-personalizes the discussion of the problem and makes it far less threatening.

It is of primary importance that readings be conducted in a one-on-one environment, free of interruption, without any trace of punitive attitude or condemnation from the reader. Probably the subject's problems have been exacerbated instead of helped by the days, weeks, possibly years of finger-wagging endured before he or she came to the reading. In this secure and non-blaming environment, the subject knows no interruptions will be tolerated and that revelations are as private, as confidential, as a discussion with a psychologist or a priest.

The original history of the tarot is shrouded in mystery. Some say it was a game played on a board; others that it was developed as a means of communication in polyglot market centers of earlier ages. The only thing we know for sure is that there is still extant a fragmentary pack dating from 1360 C.E.

There are literally hundreds of different sets of tarot cards. Almost any metaphysical bookstore will offer a wide selection of them for sale. It is wise for the beginner to buy a deck of tarot cards for which there is an accompanying book of explanation. Thus many people start with what is known as the Waite deck. In it the symbology is clear and easy to understand. In the beginning, avoid more arcane decks. They are difficult to read. As you develop, you may want to obtain and use other decks.[1] Gavin's personal favorite is the Grimaud Gipsy deck.

There have been many rectifications or corrections of the tarot pictures over the years; and although many occultists wax emotional over these changes to the cards, they are totally unimportant when it gets down to the business of a reading. The meaning of the card to the subject and to the reader at the time of the reading is the only thing that matters. If the reader memorizes an inflexible interpretation of each card, the reader is relying completely on psychokinesis happening during the shuffling, cutting, and selection of the cards. Some readers seem to rely on this method; they are less successful, however, than the readers who rely on psychokinesis plus more flexible interpretations of the cards' symbology. The cards provide an intimate contact between reader and subject, and the reader must insist on pausing during the reading to allow the messages of the unconscious to come through and reinforce the mundane impressions received through the physical senses. Without rigidly memorizing the specific symbology of each card, their general meanings can be learned. With the briefest of practice, the reader can interpolate significances of each card to give a reading that is enormously helpful to the subject.

---

[1]Gavin's personal favorite is the Gipsy deck published by B. P. Grimaud. This deck can be difficult to obtain.

The Tarot Deck

There are two types of cards in a tarot deck. There are 56 cards in four suits, closely resembling the "spot" and "face" cards in a standard bridge deck. These 56 cards are called the minor arcana. The names of the four suits will vary from deck to deck, but the most common set you will find will have suits called cups, coins/pentacles, swords and wands. The other 22 cards in the tarot deck are called the major arcana. They are set apart from the four suits.

The Major Arcana

If you lay out the major arcana in sequence and let your mind move through them, as you progress from Zero (the Fool) through XXI (the World), you see that you are progressing through life and through a spiritual realm. Because of this, many cabalists correlate the tarot cards to the paths of the Sephiroth. If it helps you understand the subtleties of the cards, you, too, should use the Tree symbology in working with the tarot.[2]

0 — The Fool: The Fool can be compared to a babe newly born. He is blithe and happy with little or no knowledge of the world. Usually the card depicts him ready to step off a cliff while a dog barks behind him to urge him on. Sometimes he carries a sack that contains his race memories.

Basic divinatory meaning: A serious choice is ahead that must not be rushed.

Reversed: There are dangers that you have not observed.[3]

---

[2]A helpful book is *The Kabbala* by Charles Ponce (Wheaton, IL: Theosophical Publishing House, 1978). It is difficult to find, however, and not available from our School library.
[3]As the cards are dealt, they can come out the right way up or reversed.

I—The Magician: The Magician symbolizes psychic powers that control the whole world. Usually the card shows a Magician in the act of controlling all the other suits. It is also the awakening of the Fool's awareness.

Basic divinatory meaning: Skill and mastery of a subject lead to positive results.

Reversed: Mastery will lead to destruction or to destructive abuse of power.

II—High Priestess: The High Priestess shows balance and passivity. The card usually shows a seated young woman in the robes of Isis. Columns on the card support the heavens. Here Isis is not necessarily the All-Mother; she can be the Temptress. Sometimes the Priestess is veiled. To gain knowledge, the Fool must penetrate the veil.

Basic divinatory meaning: There is something hidden in the future; especially there are unsuspected or unknown forces at work. When faced with this, the reader must divert and attempt to find out what these forces are before continuing with the reading.[4]

Reversed: Acceptance of the obvious can be dangerous. Short-term sexual satisfaction diverts the subject from his or her goals.

III—Empress: The Empress is Mother Nature herself, the All-Mother, female and fertile. She's very earthy.

Basic divinatory meaning: A lustful relationship with another person (or job) will bring success and much earned wealth.

Reversed: Fear of getting involved leads to inaction and poverty.

---

[4]See Zodiac Circle Reading on page 157.

IV—The Emperor: He is the male counterpart of the Empress: domineering, positively generative, often represented in a very phallic manner. He is usually shown sitting in a sterile background to show that by himself he can generate nothing. He may be the lord and commander of either a mundane situation or an emotional situation.

Basic divinatory meaning: Control, command. All subsequent cards are under his control unless they are of a higher number.

Reversed: He indicates much confusion and immaturity; in other words, everything is out of control.

V—The Hierophant: Here is the traditional teacher; the Fool must accept the teachings before he can continue. The Hierophant teaches not only mundane things, but also the higher mysteries. Often he is shown with students kneeling in supplication before him, and with pillars of wisdom by his side.

Basic divinatory meaning: A need for further study. When faced with a problem, fall back on traditional wisdom rather than new.

Reversed: An unconventional approach will solve the problem. There is something wrong in the teaching you have received.

VI—The Lovers: Sexual attraction between the two lovers is held subordinate to spiritual growth. The Fool must learn that understanding of sex leads to spiritual growth. A balance between lust, affection, and spirituality must be maintained.

Basic divinatory meaning: Choice is offered between a low path and a high one. A median, balanced path should be followed. The attractive choice may be taken, provided there are higher-level rewards.

Reversed: A wrong choice is about to be made. Unhealable rifts are indicated between lovers or a married couple.

VII — The Chariot: The Chariot can be likened to the body and the Charioteer to the mind or the will. Here you see the Charioteer in firm control of the chariot he is driving. His will controls what turns he will make in his life, and he controls the diverse forces that pull him along.

Basic divinatory meaning: Success is achieved by relentlessly following the selected path. Now is not the time to change direction.

Reversed: Crash, for the project will fail and the future will be catastrophic.

VIII — Strength: The card usually depicts someone or something weak overcoming an obstacle. Typically an inadequate young woman firmly closes the mouth of a lion. Strength, but strength gained through higher conscious awareness.

Basic divinatory meaning: The one with spiritual awareness will overcome any material obstacles.

Reversed: Material obstacles will win; another path should be followed.

IX — Hermit: For once numerology and the tarot coincide. The Hermit is someone to be looked up to, someone who guides the way to greatness. The Fool has gained absolute wisdom by climbing the peaks.

Basic divinatory meaning: Guidance will be obtained either spiritually or from meeting someone with more knowledge of your problem.

Reversed: Refusal to accept guidance results in disaster.

X — Wheel of Fortune: Here you see the fairground Wheel of Fortune spinning out your destiny. Typically the wheel is superimposed on all the other cards or on the four Elements.

Basic divinatory meaning: Good fortune; prosperity; an unexpected win.

Reversed: A sudden loss.

XI—Justice: Justice is the higher representation of the High Priestess. Again you see the pillars and the veil. This is spiritual justice. It has nothing of the earthy Isis figure about it. It can be stern with those who refuse its knowledge.

Basic divinatory meaning: A fair settlement will be reached. If you go into a negotiation honestly, you will be treated fairly.

Reversed: Beware, for someone is trying to cheat.

XII—The Hanged Man: This is the figure of a man hanging upside down—but he is alive and well. Often the face or the head expresses spiritual awareness and enlightenment. Sometimes water is prominent in this card, so you know the card is for the mind, not for the body.

Basic divinatory meaning: You should change your way of thinking about a problem. A spiritual enlightenment will lead to a better view of your problems.

Reversed: Continued attention to only the mundane world will lead to more problems instead of fewer. Continued attention to the exact, rigid meanings of the cards will lead to an inaccurate prediction.

XIII—Death: The armored knight has a skull for a face. The armor is black. The knight depicts all the nightmarish terrors that come in the dark sleepless hours. His horse treads on kings and queens; all fall down before him.

Basic divinatory meaning: A dramatic, sometimes destructive, change leads to success. Occasionally a spiritual rebirth is indicated.

Reversed: Failure results from fear of a major change in lifestyle or thought. Evasion results in disaster.

XIV—Temperance: A spiritual being pours essence of life from one chalice to another. The spiritual being is usually shown with the divine fire (represented by a triangle) within the stone of the body (represented by a square). Often a path is shown between a wasteland and a flowered garden.

Basic divinatory meaning: By careful handling of a fluid problem, you can follow the path to eventual success.

Reversed: The problem is insoluble. No matter how carefully you handle it, you will lose something of great value. Try another approach.

XV—The Devil: Here you see the symbol of the Knights Templar: the horny, horned, cleft-footed Devil. Often male and female figures are loosely chained under his command. It is obvious that the chains could be removed. Sometimes a reversed pentagram or triangle is shown either on the Devil's forehead or on the genitalia. Occasionally his phallus is enlarged and the tip broken.

Basic divinatory meaning: Where material matters and lust dominate the spirit, failure leads to violence.

Reversed: Spiritual understanding and the disciplined unchaining of lustful impulses lead to success.

XVI—The Tower: A Tower is struck down from above. The lightning flash is a revelation from God which throws people out to their deaths. This is the flash of inspiration which kills old ideas, and the flash in which truth is revealed.

Basic divinatory meaning: Change your existing approach. Selfish ways must yield to enlightenment.

Reversed: Often, the path being followed will lead to the law courts and possible imprisonment. Again a change of path is called for with a new, enlightened approach.

XVII—The Star: A young girl in a natural state trusts in the power of the Star. Often she is shown tasting water from a pool or pouring water onto seeds. This is Mother Nature before she was weighed down with worry, creating the world.

Basic divinatory meaning: New life can be engendered in old projects. The smallest seed idea can be brought to flower, provided there is a little faith in the power of the subject.

Reversed: "It won't work." An attitude of mind that says, "Nothing will succeed, especially nothing new."

XVIII—The Moon: Often shown both full and new, the Moon looks down on a scene of someone or something striving toward it. Sometimes there is phallic symbolism with a scorpion or a lobster crawling out of the sea. It is obvious that the energies from the various phases of the moon are powering the scene below and making the animals respond.

Basic divinatory meaning: Trust in your dreams and your intuition. Your intuition will lead you around an unknown enemy.

Reversed: Problems will be encountered; they will take a great deal of force to resolve. The job you will take will stifle your imagination.

XIX—The Sun: The Sun's life-giving energy brings all things into balance, and allows even a child to ride or walk in balance and to control plants and animals.

Basic divinatory meaning: Happiness, balance, and good fortune. Almost any project will succeed.

Reversed: Something is out of balance, and that balance must be restored before success can be achieved.

XX—Judgment: The spiritual judge views human subjects—men, women, children. The people are not afraid but look upward with hope.

Basic divinatory meaning: A positive change in the future, especially in your level of personal awareness. With the change in awareness comes success.

Reversed: A fear of aging and a fear of poverty in old age lead to short-sighted decisions that result in the very thing you dreaded.

XXI — The World: Having progressed through all the cards, the Fool can now dance the Dance of Life. Usually the four Elements (or the Four Horsemen of the Apocalypse) are shown under the Fool's feet. A wreath symbolizing Mother Nature's approval often appears on the card. The card represents the final achievement of a man or a woman. Here balance, both in worldly and in spiritual matters, and control of the world are won by magical and mundane means.

Basic divinatory meaning: The project will be completed and the reward, whether in gold or in spiritual awareness, will be yours.

Reversed: Stubbornness and inaction, refusal to learn the Fool's lessons, lead to failure.

The Minor Arcana

The other tarot cards are divided into four suits of 14 cards each, which closely resemble those in a standard deck of playing cards. The card that is added is the Page, who can be either male or female. Suits are Wands (clubs), Cups (hearts), Swords (spades), and Pentacles (diamonds). Within each suit the cards have similar meanings as they progress from 1 through 10 and on to the Page, Knight, Queen, and King. Let us look first at the meanings of the suits and then at the meanings of the individual cards.

You should try to memorize Table 10 on page 148–149. It is your quick reference to the significance of each card in the minor arcana.

Wands: This is the male, thrusting phallic suit associated with fire. It is the most thrusting and enterprising of the suits. Change is always foretold by a Wands card; only after you have done the layout can you tell whether the change will be for the better. In general, though, Wands are thought of as creative, since they are usually depicted as living branches rather than as dead, inanimate clubs. Thus they indicate not only the power of the cudgel but also the power of renewal. In the more phallic decks the wands are shown as penises.

Cups: Cups indicate fullness and overflowing happiness. The Cup is usually filled with water, referring to placidity, love, and knowledge. This is placidity in the bodily sense, not necessarily in the mind.

Pentacles: Here is money in abundance and wealth of all types. The five-pointed star depicting the Craft leads one to attainment of financial wealth and a wealth of spiritual serenity. All the senses are abundantly served, and the whole is harmonious.

Swords: This is the male, aggressive suit. Swords augur disaster. When held as the Christian cross, the sword still is not sheathed. At any moment it may be used to strike out and transform a situation. Hate is the key word always associated with swords and with the cross.

Table 10. Significance of cards in minor arcana.

Card	Wands	Cups	Pentacles	Swords
Ace (news)	of opportunity	from loved one	of money	of sickness, disaster, tricks
2 (work)	scientific, artistic	toward pleasure	hard work for money	overwork
3 (partnerships)	business partnership	love match	moneyed marriage	divorce, or business breakup
4 (reward for past work)	benefit through a will, or reap a harvest	gain thru sudden arrival of old friend	a raise	temporary loss; rest before battle
5 (good luck)	good business success	new devoted lover	great gain in wealth	conquest of enemies
6 (slow improvement)	businessman gives donation; new awareness of arts	old love affair ripens	non-profit org gains thru small donations	avoiding the battle
7 (upheaval, greed)	write about new subjects	costly changes in housing	change job may bring small financial success	present plans fail; beware accident

Table 10. Significance of cards in minor arcana (continued).

Card	Wands	Cups	Pentacles	Swords
8 (balance tips either way)	tact to win through	avoid divorce: spend time with loved ones	settle out of court	loss of prestige, business difficulties
9 (beautiful future)	new reliable friendships	wish of heart comes true	investments rewarded	failure, strife, delay, misery
10 (positive change)	social advancement	propety values improve; relationships too	investments improve	financial ruin; heavy burdens
Page (youth)	slip of tongue turns to gain	new pet or child	advancement for young person	aggressive young spy
Knight (new thoughts)	plan carefully for future	thoughts of love	think about money and employees	inaccurate thoughts foster quarrels
Queen (woman in authority)	pay attention to wise woman	stern woman becomes lover	follow business-woman's advice	jealous distrust or widowhood
King (man)	pay attention to wise older man	unexpected passion from older man	heed advice of businessman; or promotion	reject advice of obstinate lawyer

The Influence of Card Numbers in the Suits

The value of the card in any suit modifies its meaning. Just as the numbers of the major arcana are important, so are the numbers in the minor suits. In general, reversal of the card indicates a simple reversal of its meaning.

The Ace = News
Wands: There will be news of an opportunity.
Cups: News from a loved one.
Pentacles: News of money.
Swords: News of sickness, disaster, or trickery.

2 = Work
Wands: New work of a scientific or artistic nature.
Cups: Work toward pleasure.
Pentacles: Hard work for money.
Swords: Overwork.

3 = Partnerships
Wands: A business partnership.
Pentacles: A moneyed marriage.
Cups: A love match.
Swords: Divorce or the breaking up of a business venture.

4 = Reward for past work
Wands: Benefit through a will, or bringing in a harvest.
Cups: Gain through sudden arrival of an old friend.
Pentacles: Your wages are paid (a raise).
Swords: Temporary loss; resting before a battle.

5 = Good luck
Wands: Good business success.
Cups: A new devoted lover.
Pentacles: Great gain in wealth.
Swords: Conquest of enemies.

6 = Slow improvement

Wands: New appreciation of the arts; the businessman gives a donation.
Cups: Ripening of an old love affair.
Pentacles: A non-profit organization gains through small donations.
Swords: Avoiding the battle.

7 = Upheaval (greed)

Wands: You will write or type about new subjects.
Cups: Changes in domestic life to do with housing will be costly.
Pentacles: A change of job, and perhaps of place, may bring small financial success.
Swords: Present plans will fail. Beware of an accident.

8 = A balance that can go either way

Wands: Much tact is required to win through.
Cups: Time spent at home with loved ones will avoid divorce.
Pentacles: Avoid speculation; settle any lawsuits out of court.
Swords: Take great care in any move, for all moves lead to loss of prestige and to business difficulties.

9 = Beautiful future

Wands: New reliable friendships.
Cups: Your wish will be fulfilled in matters of the heart.
Pentacles: Investments will be rewarded.
Swords: Failure, delay, misery, and strife.

10 = Positive change

Wands: Social advancements.
Cups: Property values improve. The one who was previously fickle is now devoted.
Pentacles: Gold, silver, and other investments improve.
Swords: Financial ruin; heavy burdens.

Page = Youth, immaturity
Wands: A slip of the tongue by a stranger results in gain.
Cups: A new pet or child.
Pentacles: Advancement for a young person, either the subject or someone working for the subject.
Swords: The pushy aggressive young upstart who brownnoses the boss and can be thought of as a spy.

Knight = New thoughts
Wands: Thoughtful planning for the future is required.
Cups: Thoughts of love intrude on all else.
Pentacles: Careful thought about money and employees is required.
Swords: Thoughts which may be inaccurate lead to quarrels and dissension.

Queen = Women in authority
Wands: Attention should be paid to a poised wise woman.
Cups: The stern woman turns into a patient lover.
Pentacles: A businesswoman's advice should be carefully followed. If a businesswoman is the subject, she will be advanced.
Swords: Jealous distrust of another woman; sometimes means widowhood is imminent.

King = Men
Wands: Pay attention to a wise older man.
Cups: Unexpected passion from a stern man.
Pentacles: Advice of a successful businessman should be taken; or advancement for a successful man.
Swords: The obstinate lawyer's advice should be rejected.

The Tarot Reading

First you (the reader) sift through the deck of cards and select three or four that are appropriate both to the subject and to the question under consideration. Lay these face downward before the subject and ask him or her to discard the two that don't "feel good." The subject may touch the cards with the fingertips or may allow his or her hand to wander slowly above them. Instruct the subject to use the secondary or receptive hand for this operation; that is, the hand the subject does not use when writing.

Then look at the throw-away cards, and you will begin to get a feeling as to the subject's dislikes. Now ask the subject to select the card with which he or she feels most comfortable. Look at it and compare it with the two cards he or she threw out. Occasionally you will find that one of the discarded cards is clearly more appropriate to the question than the last card chosen. You should use the most appropriate card as the first card of the reading (called the Significator). If the last card selected was not appropriate, you know the subject feels very negative about everything, and you must take that into account in the reading. A person of this type will reject everything you say. (Once in a while you can get a better reading for such people by giving only reversed card meanings; for their rejection of the reversal will lead them to the most satisfactory result in spite of all they can do.) You are the wise reader, and you are in control of the information you provide.

Figure 28 shows the Celtic Cross layout of the tarot cards. It is a very simple and effective way of divining. The Significator is placed in the center (so it is an upright position to you, as the reader). While the Significator is being contemplated thoughtfully by both parties, the subject shuffles the remaining cards. Instruct the subject to reverse some of the cards as he or she shuffles (turning the cards from top to bottom) so some of the cards will come up reversed during the course of the reading. Let the subject finish shuffling, then cut the deck three times to the subject's left with the secondary hand. While the subject is shuffling, he or she should concentrate on the question that you both have agreed is to be the topic of the reading.

With your own secondary hand, pick up the cut deck, being sure to pick up the three piles in the direction in which they were laid down. Place the stack on the table before you; pick up the top card, turn it over, and use it to cover the

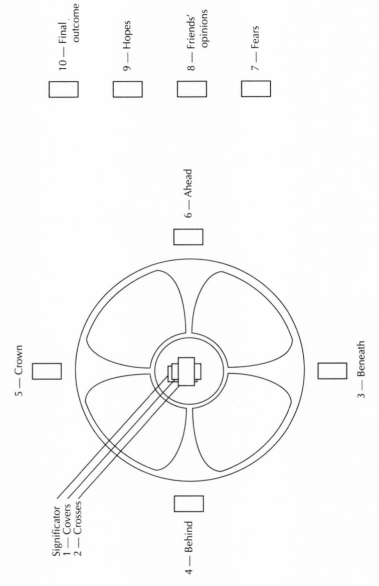

Figure 28. The Celtic Cross tarot spread.

Significator. The turning up of the card is extremely important. You must turn it over and lay it down in the same direction it had on the pack before you. Do not flip the card over end to end, since that would reverse all the cards. If it is more comfortable to flip the cards over in a head-to-toe movement, you may do so — provided you always do it and never make a change. Otherwise, pick up each card face down, rest it on one LONG edge, and let it fall face up so it is not turned top to bottom.

The card covering the Significator covers it and shows the forces that are in operation — both good and bad. Lay the next card across the covering card in a transverse position. This is the "crossing" or the preventive card. It shows the forces that oppose the subject's wishes; it is always read as if placed right way up to you.

Next deal four cards: one below the Significator, the next to the left of the Significator, the next above it, and the last to its right. The card below shows the Foundation or the basis for the problem facing the subject. The card to your left shows the Past; the card to the right shows the Future. The card above, often the most difficult to read, is sometimes called the Crown. It shows present influences, vaguely formed thoughts, and all the things that may come into being. Note particularly the word "may," because this card must be read in conjunction with the card of the Future. Perhaps a subject is thinking of a specific course of action; this will show in the Crown card — but the Future card may show an entirely different prospect. In such a case you should advise the subject to put away the thoughts and to proceed more directly toward the Future card.

Now lay out four more cards in a vertical row to the right of the cross, working away from yourself toward the subject. The card closest to you represents the negative thoughts and problems that will be associated with a given course of action from the subject's point of view. The next card represents the thoughts, opinions, and influences of family members (or business associates) regarding the subject's possible course of action. The third card tells whether the subject's hopes and aspirations will overcome the two cards below. It is especially important here to observe whether this card is a higher number than the two cards below it or one of the major arcana, rather than of a minor suit or of a less-powerful number. The more powerful this card, the more likely will be the subject's success in the endeavor.

The fourth card, closest to the subject, is the over-all Outcome. It may be that the subject will be successful in the project under consideration, but that the over-all outcome will not be positive. Almost any combination is possible: positive outcome, negative result; negative outcome, positive result; etc., etc. This is the final choice card. With your guidance, the subject must decide whether the game is worth the candle.

Detailed Zodiacal Circle Reading

At any time during the reading the subject may want a detailed examination of a specific point. When this is requested, it is customary to deal out from the undealt pack the next twelve cards in a circle that represents all the possible aspects of the problem. This circle can easily be correlated with the houses of the zodiac. Figure 29 shows such an arrangement. In laying out the twelve cards, it is traditional to start at the 9 o'clock position (think of the face of a clock) as shown in the figure, and to lay them out counterclockwise.

The moment your subject requests a clarification on any card, you should transfer over and lay out twelve cards for the zodiacal circle. When consideration of the circle is completed, you may return to the original reading and resume analysis of the cards that form the Celtic Cross.

·   ·   ·

The tarot works best when the subject is really in genuine need of an answer. Occasionally a reading will take off

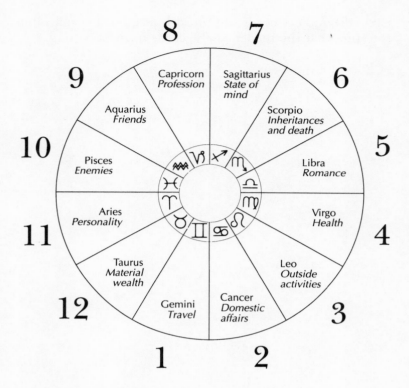

Figure 29. Zodiacal tarot layout. Note: Numbers refer to order of laying down cards.

by itself and give unexpected and very accurate results; in such a reading, the subject's feedback is hardly required, for the reader who has any sensitivity to the cards will sense the rightness of what is happening. For this reason you should be very careful about giving readings in a party setting. Many times the cards will reveal information that the subject has assumed—and now urgently wishes—was secret. Time and again we have seen the tarot used as a party game. Beware such attitudes in people who request your readings, for they can cause problems. Many people seeking a tarot reading have a secret. If the cards will reveal the secret, the subject needs to protect himself or herself, often protesting that the reader or the cards must be wrong.

Chapter 9

Palmistry

In the center of the famous Oxford Colleges in England stands the world-renowned Ashmolean Library. The founder of the library, Elias Ashmole, was the author of the earliest extant document on the analysis of the palm. Little has changed in the conclusions he drew more than 300 years ago. His work was so highly regarded that he became the Warden of the Oxford Colleges; and even under Oliver Cromwell's austere Puritan rule no one questioned his mystical work.

Palmistry has many names: cheirognomy, cheiromancy, dermatoglyphics, hand analysis, print analysis, etc., etc. The ancient Gypsy palmist holds the gordo[1] who uses a euphemism for this art in as much contempt as a Witch holds the cowan[2] who practices Witchcraft and calls it Christianity.

In medicine the palmist has shown that the simian line does actually denote a possibly mongoloid child, and is present right from birth. Many police forces have learned from Bevy Jaegers' courses how to determine possible criminal tendencies through reading palm prints and fingerprints. We admit that in these cases a euphemism for palmistry is permissible; for neither the FBI nor the medical research faculty could tolerate the term palmist. Yet they

---

[1]Everyone other than a Gypsy.
[2]Everyone who does not practice the Craft.

practice the same art as does the Gypsy in her tent: an art that traces its heritage back to the time no one can remember, while elements of this art make up the powerful Chinese healing system of acupuncture.

It was with the advance of print-taking and recording, both fingerprints and palm prints, that modern hand analysis came into its own; for those stored prints showed clearly that as we progress through life, our palm prints change. With current techniques, analysis of prints can reveal weaknesses, strengths, illnesses in the mundane and the mental makeup of individuals. It is from these bases that the palmist extrapolates the future. The jury is still out on whether or not the lifeline does this extrapolation automatically for the palmist. We tend to think that it does, in fact, show the path forward through all the opposing forces of life. Print series taken by medical research centers in Russia clearly show changes in the lifeline as a patient passes the crisis of a major illness. As the sands shift around it, in other words, the rivulet of life is moved and takes new courses across the palm.

Knowledge at a Distance

In this section we will emphasize the use of palmistry at a distance, because this is the way you will most often employ it. When you look across a room and wonder whether that Someone would make a good friend, or when you are introduced for the first time to a new acquaintance, you can tell a great deal by a single glance at the hands. The first thing to notice is the color of the skin, especially inside the palm. Is the skin color normally pink? white? sunburned? Does it display an out-of-doors roughness? Does it show a person who is very self-centered? When the skin is carefully protected, its owner prefers to be cut off from the world. The very pale cast with blue veins visible clearly shows a lack of physical energy — which is often compensated for by a lot of nervous energy. The white-handed maiden is not the lover in the poem; she is rather the chaste one who hints but does not consummate.

A yellowish cast shows the presence of an illness or the impending onset of one. A pink palm is energetic and positive. A reddish palm is that of the aggressive male, and the roughness indicates the type of work he does. The smooth, soft hand is that of the indoor office worker, and the harder rougher hand is that of the outdoor manual laborer.

Next you need to glance at the roots of the fingers to see how they are arched. Understanding the shape of the palm comes through understanding the way the fingers are mounted on it. If they run in a smooth arch, this indicates a strong balanced person without aggressiveness, with balanced interests in many subjects. When the two outside fingers are set low, there may be an inferiority complex with a lot of self-deprecation and unsureness. When the fingers are all set in a line at the same height, the person is confident, trusting personal judgment rather than taking advice from others. This person's greatest happiness lies in a job where he or she can control other people.

Shape of the Palm

As many as seven different palm shapes are defined and recognized by experienced palmists, but in this work we will limit our discussion to the four most common shapes. No one hand exactly falls into any tidy category. It is the palmist's art and wisdom which defines the basic shape and considers ways in which other shapes modify it. Some general definitions are as follows:

The Square Hand: The palm simply looks square, with the boundary from the first finger through the thumb approximately parallel to the other edge and the width across the palm under the fingers having about the same measurement as the base of the little finger to the wrist. This is the hand of the well-balanced worker who maintains a balance between practical labor and mental stability. A small square palm on a woman denotes a successful homemaker. Depending on the thickness and resilience of the hand, you see how much energy the person devotes to practical, materialistic occupations. The more solid the hand, the more solid the moral convictions and certainty about the place in life. The hand may curve outward between the base of the little finger and the wrist; this is called a creative curve. The wider the curve, the more creative is the person.

The Spatulate Hand: Here the hand is wider at the base of the fingers than at the wrist. The whole hand is rather flat and spade-like. Such a hand signifies a strong wish to shovel the money in. Yet most times people with this hand type are not interested in money for its own sake; they would rather use it to acquire material objects of wealth, especially land and houses. This is also the hand of the inventor, for the spatulate hand has a great deal of manual dexterity. In a woman's hand it reveals a great ability and affinity for delicate handcrafts; knitting and needlework are particularly indicated if the finger tips are flattened. Note: These people's wants are satisfied by the acquisition of handcrafts as much as by the crafting of materials themselves.

The Conic Hand: This is the opposite of the spatulate hand, broader at the base than at the fingers. It is the hand of imaginative people, those who are more interested in the philosophy and theory of things than in actually doing them. Often when faced with a problem that involves actually doing something, these people will make excuse after excuse and eventually get someone else to do it. Such people make great teachers. The more conic the hand, the more enthusiasm is manifested. A combination of the Conic and the Spatulate gives the "pointed hand" so admired in women. This is the hand of decorative types: neither active doers nor philosophers, they appreciate beauty and like to be surrounded by it. Your cosmetologist probably has a hand of this shape, and it is in professions of this type that such people are happiest. They must avoid arduous work or thinking, for they are not good at either.

The Long Rectangular Hand: This extension of the square hand is often found in city dwellers. The balance is excellent between the philosophical and the mental. There is a definite preference for indoor work and for indoor artistic hobbies. If the hand lacks in substance, these people will do many things they think they should, using a great deal of nervous energy. In this case the hands will be heavily lined.

The Fingers

Thousands of finger sizes and types are possible. These attributes are used in a full palm reading; the position of the fingers relative to one another is also taken into account, and the reader considers whether or not the fingers themselves are straight or bent. In the following relatively quick overview, we have not been able to take into account all the possible finger types and combinations, but have given you a good foundation on which to build your own knowledge.

The fourth (little) finger: Look first to see how close this finger lies to the other fingers. The further it points away, the more independence is manifested. If, on the other hand, it leans strongly against the third finger or even hooks under it, there is a lack of love and a wish to be brought into the family fold or into the group. It shows dependence rather than independence. If it is straight, this guarantees straight dealing. Owners of straight fourth fingers will worry themselves to death if there is a suggestion of crookedness in a deal. The little finger that points toward the third finger frequently indicates the nurse type. These people will give up their own secret desires to help others and to create happiness around themselves. A very strong kink in the last phalange of the finger, especially when it occurs on both hands and is not the result of a single injury, indicates the burglar. These people are so dependent on other people that they steal the possessions of others.

The third (ring) finger: This is usually considered to be linked with artistic ability. A strong, straight finger shows people who can appreciate beautiful things intellectually, yet are not moved by them. A slight bend toward the second finger brings more happiness. If the finger is long and thin and has an unused appearance, there are great instincts toward artistic pursuits. If the finger appears both unused and actually dead, such pursuits have been frustrated. It is good to recommend that these people at least start on their dreams, even if it be only as a hobby. A very long third finger that has the same thickness as the second finger depicts a gambler — people who take chances and who often back lost causes. If this finger is short, its owner is a doer and an achiever.

The third finger can also tell you a lot if you look at the length of the different sections or phalanges. If the base phalange is long, these people like a comfortable house. A long middle phalange indicates an appreciation of orthodox natural beauty and color; anything well made is much appreciated. The upper phalange, if thin and long, goes with an eye for a beautiful line. If sturdy, it tends to mean a gift for color balance. If the pad is well developed, there will be a developed sense of touch and an understanding of texture. A significant turning of the ring finger toward the second finger shows that mundane responsibilities have been too heavy. Some farmers locked onto the land show the ring and middle fingers firmly held together while the little finger stands well away from the dullness thus portrayed.

The second (tallest) finger: This is the center of the hand. It stands for self in relation to property, career, and responsibility. If it is long in proportion to the other fingers, it indicates aloofness — solitary people. If it is very narrow, again in relation to the other fingers, it can indicate antisocial tendencies, people who care little for the effect of their actions on those around. Such a finger is often found in research scientists who are interested only in research, not in its possible effect on the world. A very short finger belongs to gregarious people. It is seen in strangers living in another country, like the self-exiled American groups in Mexican cities. They band together and are concerned about social relationships within the group. Many talented artists, especially those who lead a school, have this very short finger.

Now decide which is the longest phalange of the finger. A long base phalange belongs to those who are interested in Mother Earth; especially long bases belong to miners. If the padding is wide and heavy, the interest will take the form of practical work in the field. If thin and narrow, it will be teaching or philosophizing about the subject. If the middle phalange is the dominant one, there is an organizational ability shown, particularly about matters in and around the home. If this phalange is wide and heavy, there will be much food stored. If narrow and thin, there will be lots of thoughts about storing food: every book on the subject will be bought, but little practical work will get done. The nail phalange, when dominant or excessively long, indicates a great interest in philosophy and religious theory. The danger in such a phalange is that these people become intellectual snobs and cannot acknowledge other people's philosophical views. If the finger leans toward the third finger, these people are looking for more lightness and happiness in life. Very occasionally it leans toward the first finger; these people are looking for better direction.

First (index) finger: This finger stands for awareness of self in the world. It is the finger that we most often use to trace out patterns. The normal length of the index finger brings it level with the third; and it should always attain the base of the nail of the second finger. When the index finger is longer than the third, it is the finger of people who automatically gain authority — the chairperson of the committee. Perhaps because women are still making a strong conscious effort to attain such positions, this tends to show more on women's hands than on men's. A poor, short, weak first finger tends to show feelings of inferiority and a lack of self-esteem, which is often hidden by much activity. When the index finger is well-shaped and is equal to the third, these people have a good sense of their position in society and a sense of responsibility that means they will take over leadership if others fail. This is the finger of vice-presidents rather than presidents, the finger of those who work more than the leaders, crossing all the t's and dotting the i's.

Now look at the three phalanges of the first finger. The base demonstrates a great appreciation for the sense of taste. The more fleshy it is, the more it demands quantities of good-tasting food; conversely, if high and narrow, it suggests an accuracy of taste in small things and a gourmet palate. If there is a narrowness where the phalange joins the palm, there is a willingness to tolerate poor food or service when conditions require it, but expectations of and demand for good food and service when the subject pays for them. When the second phalange is long or strong, there is an aptitude for craft work — for inventiveness and for making practical improvements in life's comforts. A long nail phalange typifies the successful minister or those in careers that demand personal contact with many other people. A ring worn on this finger emphasizes the wearer's need for personal contacts and for lots of social stroking.

If the first finger leans toward the second, there is a preoccupation with the home. This is often found in dedicated fathers or mothers, who often let their own wishes be subservient to those of the home, and who find satisfaction in taking this attitude. If the first finger is held apart, it means that these people feel separated from the world. They feel like strangers when communicating with other people, for they do not think as others do.

The thumb: It is often said that the thumb controls the hand. The length of the thumb is gauged from its tip to the line of attachment to the palm under the index finger, at the base of the second phalange. In a perfectly balanced hand, the thumb is the same length as the little finger. If longer, it shows dominance; if shorter, it shows subservience. The nail phalange should be the longest; and this phalange should be longer than the phalanges of the other fingers. This insures a humanitarian control over the impulses and demands of all the other fingers.

The second phalange of the thumb is considered a gauge of the owner's habitual methods. When long, it suggests much time will be expended on thinking things out; when short, it indicates impulsive activity—actions often based on intuition rather than on reason. Arguments with people having the very short second phalange are useless, for they will only be frustrated and are bored by long discussions of any topic. If the middle phalange is thinner than the nail phalange, there is a sieving or funneling of energies and the reasoning will emerge with grace, not with heavy-handed sarcasm. If the phalange is fleshy, the argument will be reiterated time and again. The lowest phalange of the thumb, which joins into the main parts of the hand, represents life. The longer it is, the more "alive and doing" is the nature of the person.

Thumb Shapes

The over-all shape of the thumb can also be used as a guide to personality:

The conic thumb: looks a lot like a cone with a pointed tip and a rounded base, and reveals a good balance of ideas between philosophy and materialism. If the thumb is large, the balance will extend to the whole personality; if small, the balance will be lost in the controlling fingers, because this shape is not the shape of a decisive doer.

Square thumb with square tip: This is the thumb of the person who can deal justly with those around.

Spatulate thumb: This is the thumb of manual workers whose work has some craft about it. A club tip indicates workers whose approach and work is rather coarse. A very clubbed tip is called a "murderer's thumb" for those people will bludgeon their way to success.

Flexibility of the Fingers

To determine flexibility, ask subjects to place their fingertips on the table and to bend their hands backward as far as is comfortable. Look at the side of the hand; see which joints bend. If the joint between the nail and middle phalanges bends back, this indicates an intuitional acceptance of ideas. Bending at the second joint shows the play between common sense and reality. Bending back between the fingers and the palm shows a flexibility in material things. People with flexibility here can make a home anywhere out of anything and still be happy in it, happy in any job even if the pay is low.

Finger Tips

Within the framework of our belief structure, the finger tips are the site where the life force flows out of the dominant hand and into the secondary hand. In many people this means that energy flows out of the right hand and into the left; but occasionally, even in right-handed people, we find that the dominant energy hand is the left. Thus the shapes of the fingernails indicate on the dominant hand how ideas are presented to the world, and on the secondary hand how ideas are accepted. Since the nails of both hands are very similar, you are looking for very slight differences between the nails of the respective hands within the general category. For example: if someone has a square index fingernail on the dominant hand and on the secondary hand it is slightly more pointed, ideas will be carried in swiftly and directly, and will be given out more slowly and evenly; for the square tip indicates a balanced evenness, whereas the pointed tip indicates a quickness of thought and directness of action.

Spatulate tip: This shows flesh bulging on each side of the nail. Here thoughts are considered, are allowed to grow before they are accepted. Spatulate tips are a sure sign of people who like to do things and who enjoy taking things apart, both with their hands and with their minds. They are not the fingers of people who like to put things together again — little boys have spatulate tips.

Conic tip: These combine a good and quick acceptance of ideas with level-headedness.

Square tip: These belong to very careful and level-headed types. Ideas are only slowly accepted and melded with existing stable characteristics.

.   .   .

While looking at fingertips, check for droplets or hard calluses in the pads. These are associated with people who may play musical instruments, who type, etc. A small bulge or hardness on the inside of the second finger indicates those who write a great deal.

Bulging Joints on the Fingers

Bulges in the joints are caused when energies do not penetrate from one phalange to the next. They reveal an impediment to the flow. Such enlargements may occur on any finger. Between the first and second phalanges they are knots of philosophy, where ideas get blocked. A pronounced knot on the second joint is called a "knot of order." Everything has its place and everything must be in its place, no matter that the result looks terribly untidy and cluttered. A small knot is a good thing; whereas a large knot makes a person rather weird to live with, for the "proper" place to store an object is not necessarily a very practical place.

The Mounts

It is unfortunate that astrological terminology got into palmistry; however, since it did, we have to go along with it. The pad at the base of the thumb is called Venus; the area

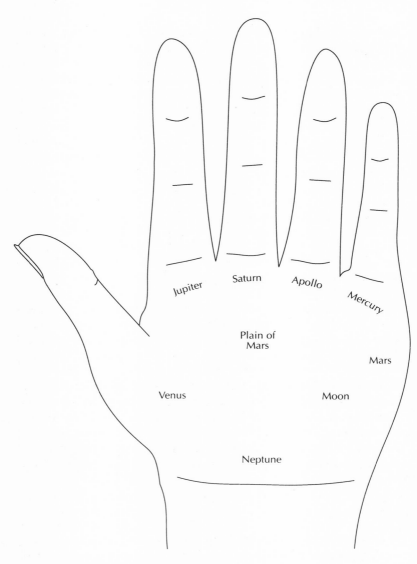

Figure 30.   The mounts of the hand.

directly opposite is the Moon. Occasionally between Venus and the Moon, at the very center of the wrist, is found a small mount called Neptune. The mount between the base of the index finger and the second finger is Jupiter; between the second and third fingers is Saturn; and between the third and fourth fingers Apollo. If this mount extends under the index finger, the outward part occasionally divides away and becomes a separate mount called Mercury. The hollow in the center of the palm is the Plain of Mars; and if there is a mount between this and the edge of the hand under the index finger, this is called the Mount of Mars. The arrangement is depicted in figure 30 on page 170. Now let us study each mount in turn.

Venus: Development of the Mount of Venus is the direct indication of people's capacity to love; it reveals the importance of love in their lives. If the mount is firm, this indicates an honest, forthright, living capacity. If it is well developed but flabby, there is some enjoyment of deviant sexual behavior and perhaps some voyeurism. The mount is flat or even hollow when people are lacking interest in the opposite sex, or in those who blush when a naughty story is told. This may also indicate a wish to withdraw from worldly contact with other people. It denotes a lack of capacity to love, even self love.

The Moon: Look how the Moon starts from the wrist and runs up the hand. The lower part embodies racial memory, merging into ancestral memory and then into childhood experiences. When the mount drops suddenly into the wrist, it shows oneness with the natural environment and with the rhythms of nature. Dancers and many people with African heritage have this sudden drop. As the mount extends firmly up, it indicates farmers and fishermen, or people who have a natural intuitive feel for cycles of the weather and for their position on the earth. If the Moon is very high and even pink-tinged, all these natural feelings are coupled with a high intuitive feeling and sensitivity. These people will be aware of the vibrations of a room and will be particularly good at dowsing. An excessively large mount belongs to worriers, who worry to such an extent that they can become mentally unbalanced. The undeveloped mount indicates people who have no feeling for cycles and vibes; consequently they cause chaos. If the mount is even slightly hollowed, these people deliberately cause and enjoy disruption of others' most sensitive feelings and emotions. Never tell a secret to someone with a mount of this type.

Neptune: This is the filling-up of the area between Venus and the Moon. It is found in charismatic, magnetic people. Good public speakers and doctors who are always being recommended have these mounts. They give out and receive tremendous energy.

Plain of Mars: Across the center of the hand is found the Plain of Mars. Since nearly all the lines of the hand traverse this area, it is the most important area for the assessment of personality. Gauge the thickness of the hand by feeling through the palm. If it is thin and the center of the palm is weak, you are holding the hand of a beggar. These people lack energy, and have no will to go out and make their own way. To get an accurate gauge of this, contrast the thickness of the palm in the Plain of Mars with the thickness through the mounts. The lack of energy is indicated by how deep the "bowl" effect is. A deep bowl indicates people who are feeble, unable to select a path through life, unable to select friends and advisors. This is the palm of dependent people, those to whom you should not give direct guidance, for they will become parasites. The firmer and higher the center of the hand, the firmer and more direct will be the path through life.

Jupiter, Saturn, Apollo, Mercury: These mounts across the top of the palm, if high and elastic, show people who have great capacity for interesting instinctive thoughts. Their minds are ever active. If the mounts are flat or bony-looking, thinking is exact and lacks emotion. Brilliant analysts have this type of flat hand, but without things to analyze they go limp; without new ideas being constantly presented, they do nothing.

When Jupiter is large, pride and ambition are indicated. If it is pointed or ridged, the pride is personal; but a well-formed, rounded mount indicates pride in family or in group, coupled with ambition and a cheerful disposition.

If Saturn is large and well formed, ambitions will be realized. Because of the striving toward this realization, these people can be moody. When things go wrong, they can become bitter and sarcastic. A small mount denotes past disillusionment and much personal unhappiness. It is found on the hand of pessimistic defeatists whose attitude is, "Nothing I can do will make any difference."

When Apollo is large, it indicates boastful people; everything is enlarged and exaggerated. A balanced, normal-looking mount indicates people with eminent good taste. An absence of the mount indicates materialistic and untrustworthy people who will do anything for monetary gain.

When the mount of Mercury is present, it indicates people who can assess their own intellectual levels. Overdeveloped, they think they are smarter than everyone else and can be bitingly witty. Underdeveloped, they think they do not have to work because native intelligence will see them through.

The Lines

The flexure lines in the hand change and move with age and with life's circumstances. First, the general character of the lines should be analyzed. Are they clear? If they are faded with many weak-looking parts, this shows either (a) a mineral deficiency or (b) people of weak, wishy-washy character. When lines are very narrow and deeply chiseled, people are intense. With very deep chiseling, single-mindedness is taken to its boring and sometimes dangerous limit. The shallower and the wider the line, the more easily swayed are these people. In the same palm, some lines may be deeply chiseled and other shallow, showing, for instance, that these people have great happiness but have no strong views on love. A hand that shows an actual dearth of lines, yet those which are present are deeply chiseled, is the hand of explorers or spies who go places that cause them physical discomfort; people with few lines are able to withstand physical discomfort and even torture. Yet they have an underlying determination and a belief in the rightness of ideas, say, or their gods. The converse of this, people with many many lines, seems to be an extreme sensitivity to surroundings and pain. In the religious theory of Witchcraft, many lines are taken to indicate people who have been reincarnated many times and will soon leave this planet plane forever.

In studying the lines themselves, you find several characteristics:

Breaks: Depending on the line where they appear, breaks can mean a severe illness, divorce, or anything that breaks the continuity of life. If the line has a long break (and especially if there is another line cutting across it), this suggests the ending of one phase and the starting of another with new ideas being brought in.

Islands: Islands appear where two paths are available. These people are ambivalent about what to do. Perhaps a woman has had, or will have, two lovers; in this case, watching the lines can show over a period of time how she swings from one to the other. Often the two paths occur when there are outside competing pressures; the reader should encourage the path that seems to be best defined in the hand.

Delta Ends to Lines: When the ends of the line look like the delta of a river, having many little branches, the energies are or will be dissipated in too many directions. The delta lines can have a finely divided yet close appearance; in this case one path will be followed, but the by-ways would have led to the same conclusion. If the lines are widely diverse, they indicate insecurity and general confusion with lack of purpose.

Cuts and Dots: Little lines cutting across the main line show inner tensions, inner conflict, and indecision, all of which hinder normal onward progress. Dots and changes of color in the lines indicate frustration and annoyance. Outside pressures are preventing the ongoing work and wishes of the personality. Color changes indicate either present or future ill health resulting from nervous frustration.

·   ·   ·

Figure 31 on page 176 shows the basic lines of the hand. Many secondary lines and fine lines are read in the science of dermatoglyphics; in the present work, however, we shall deal with only the major lines.

The Head Line

This line begins between the thumb and index finger. Halfway in between is considered to be a balanced position. When the line starts here, people will be balanced in their thinking and will discuss things without emotion. The further up the hand the line lies, and the wider the gap between it and the life line, the more independent the mind and the more selfish its owner. The high beginning indicates the impetuous youngster; the ultimate of this type is the cold-blooded ruthless murderer.

If the head line is low down and its beginning clings to the life line, thoughts are confused by too much careful thinking and sentimentality. These types are quite unable to cause any pain, even to people they don't know. They tend to do nothing; they tend to put off actions until disaster is upon them.

In the middle of the hand, the line can ride high or low, indicating a presence or lack of courage. When the line is low, people try to talk themselves out of problems; when high, they courageously go ahead. If the line arches or wavers, thoughts are lured by many encounters. If it runs straight, these people want to see straight and will take a

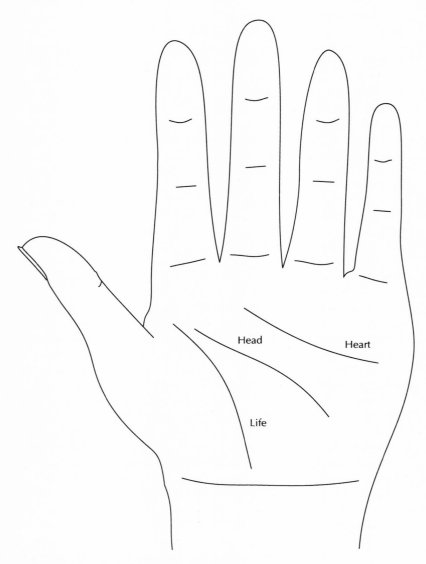

Figure 31.   The lines of the hand.

very firm path through life. In children's hands, if the line is very wavy, this should be interpreted as an indication of problems — a lack of security and strength, dominance by two or three acquaintances, an insecure world.

Look now at the end of the line. If it ends high up after a fairly straight run across the palm, the mind is cut off from the body and the person lacks warmth; every bit of feeling has been taken out of these types. If in addition it turns up under the little finger, you are looking at cold financial calculators, who, in old age, might become archetypal misers. Occasionally a little hook upward will be seen with the line coming back down again. This is the hook that Beryl Hutchinson has called the "sixpenny hook," or in America we might call it the "penny hook." These people look after pennies very carefully but are also capable of spending dollars without thought. If the line progresses across the hand and finishes low on the Mount of the Moon, thoughts will be colored by racial and ancestral memories. It is said that such people can become so disturbed by racial slurs that they will commit suicide because of them. This is especially true when the life line follows the head line across the Mount of the Moon. When the line falls down the palm quite quickly and curves around the Mount of Love, the person will be humanitarian, involved in others; and if this line too, is very long, emotionalism can lead to a youthful suicide pact.

A very short head line shows limited thought or thought restricted only to the affairs of the world. If the line is short, runs straight across, and then fades downward, this is the typical line of the businessperson. When the line shows a definite fork with one branch going downward and another going across toward the top of the Mount of the Moon, this is the writer's fork. It means that imagination and emotion can be coupled to practical ends.

The Life Line

Often the life line does not start and end clearly, so you should take care in defining its beginning and ending. It may start high up under the Mount of Jupiter, or low down very close to the thumb. When it is high, it shows ambition and a wish to do one's best. When it is low, people tend to be antisocial and withdrawn, mainly because of a lack of self-confidence. A branch may occur very early in the line when it is low, and head off into the upper part of the palm. Such a branch is an attribute of the soldier who must show courage.

The first twenty years of the line is the portion that passes under the Mount of Jupiter and begins to curve downward into the palm. This portion concerns growth and education. The line may deviate toward one of the mounts. In such a case, concern for this specific aspect has been felt. The herringbone or broken appearance at the beginning of the life line is where youngsters are absorbing many impressions. Once past majority, the line can take any of three courses:

1)   It may sweep out onto the palm;
2)   It can cling to the family line around the thumb; or
3)   It can pick a middle way and quietly encircle the lower muscles of the thumb.

The sweep and boldness of the life line show whether people can resiliently meet misfortune or whether a great deal of support is needed. The closer to the thumb it lies, the more support is needed.

As you look along the life line, you see many little branches and divisions. Observe what direction these branches take. Travel is shown by little fine long clear lines pointing toward the outside of the palm.

The ending of the life line is of primary importance. When it ends close to the thumb, it means the subject will die at home. If the line as it approaches this ending is very deep, life in the latter years will be restricted toward duty and career. The line that runs right across the palm shows that the person will live in distant places. Dips back toward the thumb show people have hidden yearnings for home;

these people are happy only when they make regular visits home.

When the lifeline ends well up on the Mount of the Moon, its owner loves adventure. If the line forks strongly, adventures will be experienced away from home and life will be divided between home and field. If the life line ends in a delta formation, energies will be dissipated at the end and the person will grow old and feeble before dying.

The Heart Line

The heart line lies above the head line. The reader will need to determine which is its beginning and which is its end; no two palmists agree on this question — so here's a good chance to use intuition. The heart line is regarded as the sentimental connection between the mundane and the mind. If the line is high and starts under the index finger, emotional force is being added to itself. If there are branches at this end, there is a great love of self. If the line continues outward across the Mount of Jupiter, emotional force is carried to the outside world; these people can direct others. If the line starts as a curve between the first and second fingers, there is a great warmth of affection toward others. If the line stops short of the Mount, affection is shared between self and the world, and these people will know both the heights and depths of emotion. A line that curves across the palm shows owners who will work continually and actively to sway the emotions of other people. If the line should cease or turn up under the other mounts, emotions will be directed to these qualities respectively. Under Jupiter they will have a great deal of self-pride. When the heart line is very short, these people have no ability to love; they can like others, but never love them.

•   •   •

In this section, we have deliberately emphasized the general, easily recognized aspects of the hand: aspects that can be seen on the TV screen or in pictures. Using these methods, even if you read only the shapes of the palms and fingers, you can assess all the people involved in a problem. We believe that this is a better way of proceeding than trying to get absolutely everything you can out of every line on the subject's hand. If you want to pursue palmistry further, of course, you can learn to take palm prints and analyze them.

The intimate contact gained through the use of palmistry is a great aid to any reader. The fact that people's innermost secrets are revealed through the hand gives the palmist a unique link to subjects, a link as close as physicians' or psychologists' link with patients. The more we study palmistry, and the more the scientific community studies it, the more factual seems to be the basis for its claims. It is a subject that repays deep and continual study, for we can read in our own hands our strengths, weaknesses, and destiny.

Chapter 10

Scrying

Grimy face, grimy hands, the smell of wood smoke, a cauldron bubbling over a fire . . . The animal is dragged in to the slaughter. Its head is hit with a solid branch and it staggers to the earth where a wizened old man cuts its throat. Soon its guts are spilled onto the floor in a steaming, slippery pile; cleaner hands feel them, wise eyes inspect them. The liver is examined, and finally all is pronounced favorable for the next year. Middle Ages sorcery? Ancient magic? No. A demonstration of how to butcher a pig in 1978 at an Ozark farm by the University of Missouri. Why were the entrails read? Very simple—the men wanted to see whether the pig had any diseases or parasites, whether its diet had been healthful. From these auspices they could predict whether next year's pig crop would be good for Farmer George.

The scryer is the one who sees into the future, who uses CC in conjunction with some device or object—even the entrails of a pig—to help "see" within. In this section we will discuss the following types of scrying:

1) the crystal ball;
2) the sand-pattern;
3) tea leaves;
4) seashells;
5) liqueur;
6) smoke;
7) candlewax.

There are many other types, too. What they all have in
common is their value as a scrying device or autoscope, as it
is called. The difference between the various methods is the
type of autoscope and the amount of involvement that subjects feel in the reader's work.

It seems to be a rule that the more subjects are
involved, the less they have to be awed by the atmosphere of
the reading. In crystal ball work, where the most subjects
may do is put a timid hand near the ball, many props are
used to convince them of the importance both of the reader
and of the revelation. Often autographed pictures adorn the
walls of the temple; the ball itself is enshrined like a holy
relic; and everything must be conducted in a reverent and
mystical manner. At the other end of the scale are shell or
liqueur readings, where the atmosphere is light and casual.

It is our belief that these behavioral patterns are not
simply coincidental, but are necessary for the success of the
method. Psychic awareness must be at its height in crystal
ball work where the reader has very few mundane clues to
work with; it is least necessary when subjects are involved
and participate more actively in the reading.

One thing that all good scrying systems require, but
which is often lacking, is that the reader use a logical
approach to the problem and decide on the path to take. It
must be a path that draws subjects along, one that enables
them to start communicating, either verbally or at an unconscious level, on topics that are not threatening. A typical
path is shown in figure 32 on page 183. Starting at the
bottom of the figure and imagining that the reading can go
in any direction as it climbs, at first the reader starts by
talking about the subject—family, friends, financial background, etc. Questions as simple as "What is your name?"
"What shall I call you?" "What do your friends call you?" or
"What do you really like to be called?" all have great significance. After a few readings these lead-in cues will come
naturally.

From this foundation the reader can go into immediate
past. "Why did you come?" "How did you get here?" "Have

you been well?" "How's the job going?" are all useful non-threatening questions. When you come to Now, the reader will try to define more precisely what the subject's question is. What is the exact problem that has brought the subject here? This is not necessarily the question the subject is asking, for he or she may not have done enough introspection to have the problem accurately defined. All the subject knows is that he or she is miserable.

It is at this point that the reader uses the chosen method to start reporting impressions and getting feedback from the subject — obstacles, hopes for the future, feelings about friends and enemies — the subject's real thoughts. Finally all of this leads to a resolution which sends the subject away, if not happy, at least with a firm resolve and some sort of path to follow.

Everyone will use different methods; everyone will have a different approach. But unless the reader has a way of narrowing in and getting to a resolution, the reading can go on forever and peter out in a fragmented and unsatisfactory way for both subject and reader.

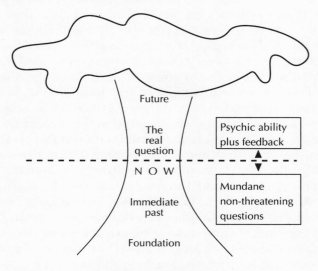

Figure 32. The path through a reading.

Crystal Ball

The ball rests on an ornate table covered with a clean and high-napped smooth velvet cloth. Black was universally popular in earlier days, but currently a very deep blue or violet cloth is preferred. A special small room or space should be set aside for the work; one very capable scryer we know always uses a tent. The reader should be smartly dressed in comfortable flowing garments. Contrary to the old stereotypes, readers wear little jewelry. Some symbol of reassurance should be on the wall behind the reader where the subject can see it. An equal-armed cross with a circle at its center seems to work for Christians, agnostics, and all. On a table in front of the cross (or other religious symbol), candles should be placed in such a position that the reader's body prevents their light from reflecting on the surface of the ball. When the subject has taken a seat opposite, the reader lights the candles to signal the commencement of the reading. It is not a good idea to use incense or perfume in the room, although a small basket or posy of mixed aromatic herbs may be placed between the candles. Autographed photographs may be placed on the walls. Certificates from high school graduation on up could also be hung on the walls. The reader's chair should be slightly higher in elevation than that of the subject so the reader can gaze down into the ball and lift the eyes only very slightly to look at the subject's eyes. Dilation or contraction of the subject's pupils is an immediate unconscious reaction that provides valuable clues both to the interest in the reading and to the acceptance of it. Above all else, make sure the room is comfortable. It should be awe-inspiring but not overpowering. During the actual reading, the candles should be the only light source.

The reader should have some means of gauging the time. A silent clock on the wall behind the subject is therefore required. A typical plan view layout is shown in figure 33. Music, noises from outside that penetrate the room, the cutting on and off of an air conditioner or furnace system, all these will distract from the reading; the more you can do to eliminate all extraneous sounds, electrical disturbances, in fact all irrelevant inputs, the better will be the atmosphere and the reading itself. The worst possible thing that can happen during a reading is for the telephone to ring and the reader come back from answering it and say something like, "Now! Where were we?" Subjects must be confident that they are absolutely the only thing on the reader's mind.

All the hints that follow should help your early readings. Once you have given a few readings, you will adjust the conditions to suit yourself. We cannot really tell you how best to see things in the ball. It is a meditative-type device that allows the unconscious to give conscious images. In other words, it allows the Consciousness Connection to work.

Gaze quietly into the ball. As you concentrate on the ball, it is usual to see first a milky, misty manifestation. The longer you gaze, the more disconnected you become from your surroundings, and the more the CC condenses the fog into significant meaningful shapes. They may form a single appearance and stay that way throughout the entire reading; sometimes when you ask a particular question, the shapes

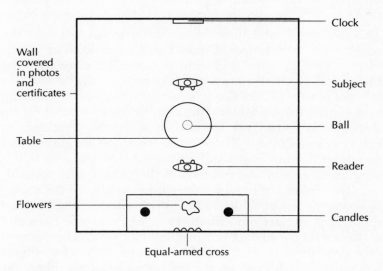

Figure 33. Typical layout for a reading room.

make sudden vivid changes. We cannot tell you what the shapes mean; for your background is different than ours. The experiences that your unconscious and conscious mind have had are entirely different from experiences our minds have had. We like to use the illustration of a seagull to point up this fact. To those who are of the Jonathan Livingston Seagull (Bach) generation, a gull symbolizes freedom and spirituality. To us who live on the coast, a gull is a bird that messes up our patios. If you see in the ball a seagull flying, what does it mean? Only you can say.

All your personal emotions must be set aside when you use the ball. While you give a reading, try to take on the emotions of the subject. It is an art that requires daily practice, not something you can pick up in the middle of a party and give readings with. If you are so psychic that you can give readings in the jangled atmosphere of a party, you don't need the ball in the first place.

Sand Patterns

The casting of sand patterns has been associated with the occult since earliest time. Colored sands are found in burials of very early people, and sand pictures are drawn by the Indians of North America and throughout the world as a focus of power. One of Gavin's earliest memories is watching how his mother—who was afraid of heights—scrambled up the cliffs at Alum Bay in the Isle of Wight, England, to gather colored sands. Those sands were cast on glass plates or placed in glass vases and varnished into place so that a permanent record was retained of the picture they formed.

In this kind of reading, the subject is offered the choice of several bowls of colored sand. With a small long-handled spoon, the subject dips whatever color he or she likes and scatters it on the surface of a black mirror which is supported on a small piece of sponge under its center. When the subject has put as much sand on the mirror as he or she likes, the base questions are asked.

Now comes the reader's art. With a small wand the reader taps the edge of the mirror. Sometimes the reader will stroke along it, sometimes flick the wand with almost enough force to break the glass. As the reader taps and flicks, the sands mix and the patterns change. If the reading is going badly, the reader hands the subject a second wand and directs him or her to tap the glass. As the reading progresses, the reader becomes more definite, pressing down on one corner or along an edge, making all the sand run in that direction. If the original patterns tend to persist, there will be little or no change in the subject's fortunes; if they seem to run and flow all over the place, however, violent early change is seen. Patterns may take on the shadowy outline of castles, houses, and rivers. The colors that the subject has used and the colors assumed by each individual pattern give the reader many clues that enable the CC to go off on the wildest flights — which, it turns out, can be precisely applied to the question being asked. Occasionally the subject will deliberately change a pattern that is obvious to both of them. When this happens, the reader should pursue that specific pattern and find out why the subject feels an aversion to it.

As with scrying, it is difficult to tell you what all the myriad patterns mean. With a little experience, you will develop your own interpretations and become an adept in this most ancient art.

Tea Leaves

With the advent of the teabag, the art of tea leaf reading has gone from our drawing rooms. To bring it back, all you need to do is break the teabag in the pot or, preferably, use loose packed tea. Loose tea works better because the pieces of leaf are larger. Those who make tea bags learned years ago that when they grind the leaf more finely, the tea is stronger and uses less leaf.

This is the cozy reading: the one done before the fire when it's dull, gloomy, and cold outdoors. Hot buttered toast, toasted teacakes and muffins, are all brought to mind when you start to do a tea leaf reading. Therefore we do not recommend that you use this type of reading when you are trying to solve the world's problems or advise someone on make-or-break business venture. Romance and little personal problems are the order here.

When the tea has been drunk and a little is left in the cup, the subject peers into the murky remains and swirls the cup with the secondary hand, making at least three full circles. Then the subject quickly turns the cup upside down into the saucer and lets it drain. Often the reader will tap the bottom of the cup with a wand or with a long pencil. During this period, the base questions are asked so when the teacup is turned over and cradled in the reader's palm they can go directly into a consideration of the problem and what the future holds.

Over the years the patterns seen in teacups have become standardized, and most readers use similar interpretations for the basic patterns that may appear. First the reader holds the handle downward to see into the cup. The handle then represents the far past; and as the reader looks at the patterns going around in a clockwise direction inside the cup, the past gives way to the present and the right-hand side of the cup indicates the future. Often there are too few patterns for a very long reading, so another cup of tea is indicated. Of course during the pouring, drinking, and the whole ritual of the second cup, more discussion of the problem takes place.

Numbers and Letters: These should be carefully noted, remembering that no way is "up" in a teacup. Each segment can be read from any direction. Thus an *m* can just as easily be a *w*, or a *d* a *p*. It is easy to confuse an s with an 8 with a 5. Because of this, these elements are usually read first, and the subject's aid is enlisted to decipher the actual symbol intended.

Lines: Lines are usually interpreted as paths. If they are short and broad, they become symbols of sex; if they have a blob at one end they are called snakes and stand for disaster caused by an unreliable person, the "snake in the grass." The road that indicates a journey is often accompanied by a snake, which indicates dangers along the way. If the road ends in a delta, the subject's energies will be wasted. If it ends abruptly, this is taken as a good sign. If the end is tee'd, the subject is traveling down a dead end. A firmly delineated road that has a long break in it, especially across the bottom of the cup, means a journey across the water by ship. If the break is toward the rim, the journey across water will be by air.

The Cat Face: This is interpreted as meaning, "Beware of a false, catty friend." If the cat seems to be smiling, it is an indication of someone pushing the subject into a venture he or she should not pursue; the cat knows what is to come, and the subject should make changes in plans.

Animals: A small circle with a tail represents a mouse. The mouse suggests the subject look to his or her reserves, for something is nibbling away at them. As the body becomes larger and the tail lengthens, the mouse transforms into a rat. This is one of the most evil, and hence the most disastrous, symbols to be seen in the cup, for it will eat a person out of house and home. A good friend, probably a woman friend, is considered to be the rat. If the body shape is a long oval, there is a male rat in your life; the oval sometimes indicates sexual misadventures. With longer legs and a short tail, the symbol becomes a horse. This foretells romance; if not a present romance, a lover will soon appear. If the horse is thin, the love will be highly romanticized and will not be consummated. If the horse is fat, beware of pregnancy; for a fat horse is earthy and lustful. A short-tailed short-legged symbol is that of the dog. Your friends will rally round, and you will receive much affection and aid from them.

Clocks and Circles: These are the most positive signs in the cup. They indicate completion; the subject's plans will come full circle and be successful. The time on a clock is very difficult to judge. Usually the cup's handle is kept down and the clock viewed as if it is upright, but if this gives a meaningless result, rotate the cup until a realistic reading of the time (which is usually taken to be a number of days) is obtained.

•   •   •

Any other symbols seen are usually taken at face value. Ships, airplanes, cars all mean travel by the represented mode of transportation. Male and female figures usually indicate that new male or female friends will be coming into the subject's life. Whatever is seen, it's all good fun and an excuse for another cup of tea. Most people don't take this seriously, but in fact tea leaf reading really does seem to work very well, and we encourage you to try it.

Sea Shells

Sea shell reading seems to be confined to people dwelling along the seashore, and most of the time it seems to be done in the winter; consequently it is a method rarely heard of. It is almost as if its practitioners are ashamed of it, or ashamed that those sophisticated people who use such things as the *I Ching* might laugh at their rustic folk ways. This is a pity, because it is a very powerful method.

In the old days a bean crock full of water was viewed by the light of a candle; but a Pyrex glass bowl or deep baking dish filled with water tinted dark green works just as well. The green is said to be the color of the sea in winter; to us it signifies the color of new knowledge and of beginnings as well.

A large pile of shells is offered to the subject; he or she is instructed to take one at a time at random and gently place them in the water. Some of the shells have holes in them; some are just broken pieces; they come in various shades from white through pink, yellow, rust brown, and black.

The shells selected indicate the subject's feeling about himself or herself. Are the shells tiny or large? Does the subject go for colors or white shells? The early selections are the feelings about self that form the basis for the present problem. As the reading progresses, the selections are taken to mean changes that must be made to face or ameliorate the problem.

Now watch carefully how the subject places each shell in the water. Is the subject careful with the shells? Or are they just thrown in any old way? Are they consistently placed in one position, or are they put in at random? All these gestures tell the competent reader how the subject will face the problem at hand. Will it be done with care or randomly? Will it be attacked furiously or handled deftly?

A shell either floats or drops to the bottom of the water. Broken shells drop quickly, indicating disruption. A floating

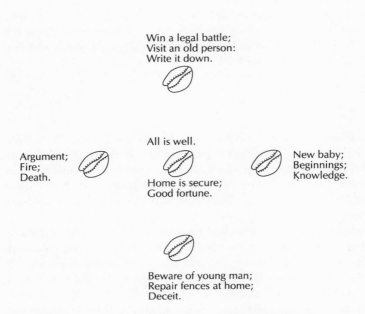

Figure 34. The meaning of locations where shells fall.

shell indicates good fortune and success: the subject will be buoyed up. The slower the shell makes its way to the bottom, the longer the time it will take for the problem to be resolved. A long and difficult journey may be indicated.

When the shell gets to the bottom, its location represents a direction in which to go. Forward is indicated by a southerly or westerly shell; an easterly shell indicates "Wait for more information." A northerly shell indicates that a visit to someone older or the reading of an old book will help. A shell that falls due south means that hard work is the only solution, and a shell that falls in the west means creativity or alternately: "Beware a tempting woman."

In a question on family relations, a shell that falls eastward is a new baby. A southerly shell means, "Repair your fences at home." A westerly shell means a violent argument, and a northerly one means the subject will win a legal battle. The central shell means, "Do nothing. All will be well." Figure 34 gives a general idea of the various meanings for shell locations. When several shells have been placed in the water, an over-all pattern will emerge. The pattern gives the final resolution of the reading.

Liqueurs

This reading is done by placing heavy cream on the surface of a liqueur, or by layering one liqueur upon another. Four liqueurs are suitable for layering—golden Drambuie, red cherry Brandy, green Creme de Menthe, and dark brown Kahlua. Since this divining method finds its home in tropic islands, this last liqueur is the one most often used with cream. The cream is made to mix with the liqueur through the use of a soda straw: the method is gently to insert the straw vertically through the cream and into the liqueur. The subject blows gently through the straw; bubbles of cream and trailing lines will be formed as the straw is removed. The patterns created take on meanings similar to those seen in tea leaves. Those that rise rapidly to the surface indicate good fortune; whereas those that lie on the bottom or immediately mix with the liqueur indicate misfortune. A short vertical line that occasionally forms with its bottom mixed and its top still clearly defined represents an unhappy love affair.

This is a popular after-dinner or party pastime; but as with tea leaves, occasionally you will find that the reading has taken off and has become painfully exact. As with all systems, the light-hearted can very quickly become a matter for tears and regrets. Many a friendship and romance has been broken by revelations that came to light through liqueur readings.

Smoke Patterns

Candle magic in all its diverse forms is a natural for divination. In earlier times during quiet candle-lit evenings, many tales must have been told as the seer looked into the flame. Nowadays we look into fire and see many patterns. Smoke patterns are clearly one of the ways in which those fleeting impressions can be recorded and read at leisure.

It is usual for the reader to have available six candles in diverse colors. These are the strong colors: white, blue, red, gold, yellow, and green. Cards about eight inches square are also available, in six pale colors: white, natural, pink, light yellow, sky blue, light green.

The reader asks the subject to select a candle and light it, then to pass a card almost horizontally through its smoke. The first card and candle signify the base, or the background to the question. Now that candle is extinguished; the subject lights another candle, selects another card, and moves the card through the smoke. This card represents the present. The whole procedure is repeated a third time; the last card represents the future. The cards are laid out with their smoke patterns uppermost in front of the reader from left to right, past to future. On each card the reader writes the color of the candle that was used to make the pattern.

Figure 35 indicates the meanings of combinations of cards and candles. The line across the center through the X's is called the Line of Balance; it shows where the card and the candle have the same meaning. The dotted line in fig. 35 is the Line of Unbalance. Above and to the right of the Line of Unbalance lies the Triangle of Intellect. This is where the subject will intellectualize the answer rather than get involved emotionally or physically. The further toward the top right corner the subject's choice lies, the more spiritual and aesthetic will be the subject's feelings about the problem. This does not mean that feelings are not deep or that they are not very important and serious; it is just that the aesthete will never do much or get very violent about anything.

The converse is true of the lower left Triangle of Emotions. As the choices tend toward the bottom left-hand corner, so physical action and even violence are the rule of the day or have played a large part in past actions. Beware of such a subject, for a single word of yours may have a violent effect on the lives of many people.

When you first look at the patterns formed on each card by the smoke, it will be noticeable that some are heavy. The

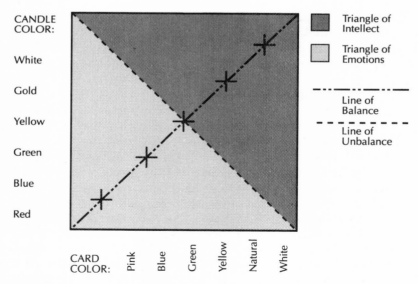

Figure 35.   Candle/card interplay.

carbon is built up on the card, and the card may even be scorched. Pay close attention to these heavy buildups and scorchings. The accumulations are called Mounds of Emotion, and any holes are sometimes called gunshots, because they denote a high level of violence. Again we can tell you very little about interpreting the specific patterns. Try to get the subject involved in seeing what he or she has done on the cards. Often the subject will see things, as a patient on a psychologist's couch sees in inkblots things that the reader would never think of. When the subject sees something very clearly, take careful note; for the subject is projecting the problem. In telling the reader what he or she sees, the subject is actually telling his or her hopes or fears.

To preserve the patterns, outline in pencil the areas where buildup of carbon is heavy; knock off the excess carbon; spray the cards with any artist's fixative and store them. On the back of the card, note the time, the date, and the outcome of the reading. Preservation of the cards in this way provides an excellent basis for this subject's next reading. With the passage of time, shaky patterns become firm or problems that were strongly shown fade into the background. Like many of these autoscopic devices, smoke patterns are a powerful predictive tool.

Wax

Patterns formed by wax dripping onto a tabletop or running down the side of a candle have been read ever since there first were candles. When a candle burns unevenly and in a wasteful manner, it indicates negativity. This interpretation probably began when candles were made at home and wasting one was expensive either in terms of labor or in money.

For divination, the choice of candles should be fat and stubby; the usual colors are white, black, red, blue, yellow, green. Make sure that you buy candles that carry their color into the wax; a white candle with an outer layer of colored material will not serve your purpose.

While the subject sits across from you, light six candles. While they burn and form a generous pool of wax at the bottom of each wick, the basis of the reading can be established. Ask which color the subject likes. Does he or she think that one candle or another is burning as well as the rest? From such simple questions can your initial character analysis be made.

In actual formation of the patterns, two methods are popular. One is to drip the wax into a bowl of water; in this case patterns are formed on the surface. The other is pouring or splashing wax onto the back of an earthenware dinner plate. We favor the use of the dinner plate. Make sure the plate is on an adequate surrounding of paper, for the wax should be poured from such a height that it will literally splash or bounce.

The subject selects the first candle and splashes wax onto the plate. Now the reader has much information. The way the wax is dropped, how central and symmetrical is the pattern, what color is selected, all give the reader clues to this first pattern, which represents the background of the pattern. In it the reader should see faint pictures representing past problems and mounds of wax that represent strengths. When this pattern has been fully explored, the subject selects another candle and splashes more wax on the back of the plate over the previous pattern. The interaction of this fresh wax with the basic pattern shows how the present has developed from the past.

If the subject uses the first candle a second time, there has been no great traumatic change. If a violently different color is selected, say a red over a white, there has been a great deal of activity and change from past to present. The reader's developed sensitivity to colors will tell what these color changes signify. In reading the new pattern, always consider how past and present interact on each other. When this part of the reading is complete, the subject chooses yet another candle to represent the future, and again splashes wax onto the existing patterns. Now the future can be seen as it rises from the past.

If the reader thinks the subject will return for further readings, break the wax carefully off the plate and store it; for it will form the basis of future layers that can be built up as the subject's life progresses.

．　　　．　　　．

Anything that forms a pattern of a random nature can be used as an autoscope, provided the subject and the reader can exercise some conscious control over its use. A mature lady who used to come in twice a week to help clean for Gavin's mother was an adept at reading stains. From what seemed like just a single glance at a spilled drink stain, she could tell who had been in the house!

Lying out on a sunny beach watching those high clouds go by can be an enjoyable experience. The Silva Mind Control folk get their students to change the cloud patterns; thus cloud reading has recently taken on a new meaning and dimension, for it has good potential as a Consciousness Control.

Start the practice of scrying with something easy like smoke or wax patterns; then graduate to the more subtle art of the crystal ball, where the patterns form at the behest of the consciousness interplay between reader and the subject. Above all, we must warn you in scrying: Do not be lighthearted or flippant. You can blame no one for destructive results but yourself. You can't say it's in the dice or in the cards—for it isn't. It is in what you make of those elusive patterns. Sometimes you will be so positive about a given set of events that you may miss the more elusive pattern and go off in a direction that may be completely wrong for the subject's life. Beware those very arbitrary statements, for scrying is a mystery. Look behind surface presentations for the underlying messages to be sure you have gotten the correct meaning. Make sure the subject understands what you are saying and agrees with it.

Chapter 11

Dreams

A nnounce at a dinner party that you are into dream analysis, or even that you had an unusual dream and you
will get more attention than the young lady who says she is a
sex therapist. Everyone knows (at least subliminally) that
dreams have great significance and everyone is interested in
understanding what is causing their sleep to be disturbed.
Don't ever doubt that dreams are just as important in your
life as they were when the first dream analyst punched
impressions into the clay tablets found later by archaeolo-
gists in Chaldea. We know now that the first dream books go
back to pre-Biblical times. In Biblical times, dream prediction was so well entrenched that it is one of the few occult
arts endorsed by the Bible, and references to the use of
dream analysis abound. Jehovah himself promised dreams
to guide old men and visions for the young. As we shall see,
the subtle difference between dreams and visions may be
said to have divided the psychological world for years; Freud
regarded dreams as wish fulfillment; and Jung saw them as a
means of integrating ancient primeval race memories with
the pressures of modern life. Are these the visions of the
young and the dreams of the old? Our view is closer to what
is called the biological school of dream analysis.

Nowadays analysis of dreams and nightmares is a
highly paid adjunct to the psychologist's work with emotionally disturbed people. More and more it is found that by
analyzing dreams with the subject's help, early traumatic

experiences can be identified and their later ill effects can be eliminated. Occasionally a dream is so effective in producing a ghastly warning that the dream itself produces a trauma. In such cases, spending thousands of dollars and hundreds of hours in the psychologist's office looking for childhood incidents would be a waste; for the incident occurred only in a dream.

Can dreams predict? Millions of documented cases show they can indeed. Abraham Lincoln's dreams are perhaps the best known; he foresaw and recorded his predictions of the outcome of many events during the Civil War; he foresaw his own assassination. Each of his predictive dreams was prefaced by a dream of a large ship sailing across the ocean and across the country to the place where he would see the event.

Many inventions have resulted from dreams, and numerous scientists give credit for some of their most spectacular discoveries to dream messages. It is well known that Thomas Edison slept in a chair in his lab so he could immediately try out any ideas he got through dreams. The discoverer of the benzene ring, Professor Kugel, got the idea from a dream; without his discovery, organic chemistry would not exist. These cases are by no means isolated. The sewing machine, the DNA molecule, and the bicycle are all documented cases of dream discoveries.

Dreams Come to Everyone

So many people told us they did not dream, that we made an extensive study of the phenomenon. Everyone dreams. The problem is that although most people dream their dreams in a visual manner, some people do not. Many investigators miss the point that dreams can be received through senses other than sight. Our percentage breakdown among the various types of awareness is approximately as follows:[1]

---

[1]Taken from an analysis of almost 2,000 student replies to a questionnaire we sent out in the 1960's.

90%	see pictures and dream conventionally;	
6%	feel things and wake up in a mood;	These people
1%	taste things and wake up with a good or a bad taste;	report:
1%	smell things — the bad-smell phenomenon;	"No dreams."
2%	hear things — somebody told me	

Making up tables for the meanings of the various feelings and impressions that dreamers get is beyond the scope of this book, because it is an area in which far too little research has been accomplished. If you get impressions during your sleep time, these are just as much dreams as the vision of people who see pictures. If you believe you are clairvoyant, but still think you do not dream, your life may be too irregular to allow retention of the fleeting visions of the night. So regularize your evening procedures — get plenty of sleep, and record your dreams.

In 1953 a new breakthrough in dream research occurred: the correlation of rapid-eye movement (REM) sleep and the symbolic dream state. In that state the subject unconsciously twitches and displays high brain-wave activity; the eyes move rapidly under their closed lids as if the subject is watching something. In fact the subject reacts as if he or she were awake and involved in day-to-day activities. Scientists currently call this D-state sleep; that is, sleep in which the subject is dreaming. In D-state, sexual arousal is frequent and orgasm occurs in dreamers of both genders. The finding that became the breakthrough was this: when people were awakened in the middle of a D-state phase, more than 94 percent could remember vivid visual imagery and could recount very detailed symbolic dream situations. The remainder could report feelings and impressions.

D-state activity contrasts strongly with the remainder of subjects' sleep time. In the remaining sleep time, called A-state, the subject is quiet, moving rarely, and has only that brain activity required to sustain life functions. When awakened from A-state sleeping, subjects report realistic, thought-like visions and feelings that resemble waking experiences. Analysis of these reports shows clearly that A-state dreams are, in fact, astral travel.

Natural sleep therefore divides itself into clearly distinguishable periods of A-state and D-state activity. Several thousand experimental studies based on the external manifestations of A- and D-state sleep show that D-state takes up about one quarter of the sleep period and A-state about three quarters. The first D-state period normally occurs 100 minutes after the onset of nightly sleep and lasts from five to ten minutes. Ninety to 100 minutes after this, another D-state period occurs, slightly longer than the first. The cyclic pattern repeats through the night with each successive episode of D-state lasting longer than the last, until in the early morning D-states as long as thirty minutes occur. When people are well rested, these early morning D-states often cause them to awaken.

D-state is not characteristic of the onset of sleep. As you drift from wakefulness through drowsiness into A-state sleep, there is a short period, called hypnogogic, when the mind reviews the activities of the day. This is a transient dreamlet state that quiets the emotions and settles the mind before the spirit is allowed to separate in its first astral travel of the night.

Figure 36 shows a typical night's sleep pattern. Notice that toward morning, especially in the time period about 3 to 4 A.M., another hypnogogic state sometimes occurs. This

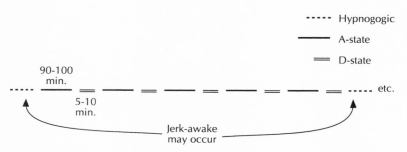

Figure 36.   Typical dream states.

is the one in which all problems loom too large. It is the dog time of the night.

If you have a timer that can control a record player or a similar instrument, set it to awaken you at various times during the night. We have found that a timer doing this is better than a beeping or buzzing alarm. The instant you are awake, write down in a notebook one or two words that are significant to what has just been happening in your mind. You will find that you really do dream. Remember, though, that the sensation may simply be one of a bad taste or of a sweet smell or Mother talking to you, or similar fragmentary dreams that are not of the visual kind. Whatever impression remains after waking, note it before it can elude you, to be considered later.

To make sure that you do dream, you must bring some organization into your life schedule. These five rules should be made a part of your pattern for successful retention of dream material:

1) Get adequate sleep. If you are tired, your sleep will be very deep and sound. When you are awakened from such sleep, the body's natural resentment prevents good recall.

2) Leave your worries behind. If you are obsessed and preoccupied by the day's worries, the hypnogogic period extends itself into your first A-state interval, so the timing of the awakening cannot be predicted as reliably as is necessary for your investigation.

3) Calm before sleep. It is best to avoid violent emotions just before sleep. Horror films, family arguments, intense study, all tend to prolong the hypnogogic period.

4) Regular bedtime — you are a creature of habit, and you can use your habits to help in accurately timing your A-state periods. If you always retire at the same time, you will go into your second A-state period at very nearly the same time.

5) Waking — you will need some form of clock-operated music-maker, for you want to be wakened by soft music; a

tape of a Chopin etude is ideal. We advise against use of a clock-radio because this could awaken you to the harsh, staccato voice of an announcer.

·   ·   ·

Notice we do not suggest that you document fully your dream experiences. A few key notes will enable you to recall the remainder of the dream the next morning, and writing down a few notes or words creates a minimal disturbance in your night instead of making the task too onerous.

A Typical Dream

I am sailing a small boat. It is a pleasant after-noon. I am naked, enjoying the sunshine. Sud-denly a commercial fishing boat comes by with a lot of people on board, and I search frantically for clothes. Soon the fishing boat has gone and it gets dark. Ahead I see a beautiful mermaid sitting on a rock. I rush below and get a blazing firebrand. I am about to hit her with the torch when a wind comes up from nowhere, the boat capsizes, and I am drowning. At this point I am so terrified that I jerk awake.

We are going to use this dream and variations of it to illustrate how variously dreams can be interpreted and why the subject must always be involved in any dream analysis.

Recurring: Let's say the dreamer is a sailor, and that the dream repeats itself with various modifications over a period of months or even years. In its first recurrence the subject is still naked but finds a life jacket to wear. The ending is still the same. In the next, as he goes over the side the subject drops his firebrand and grabs a rope, and with great diffi-culty climbs back into the boat. After several other varia-tions, the latest dream shows him in the boat naked with an erect phallus, sailing smoothly by the fishing boat. As he sails by, his new fiancee climbs into his boat, shedding her clothes as she comes. The boat overturns almost as it did in the first dream; but the dreamer and his fiancee cling together and float gently away onto a sandy beach.

This dream sequence is typical of many. One interpretation would be that the man is at first totally unprepared to go sailing. He is naked and the professionals on the fishing boat will see his nakedness and his lack of preparation. He fears their scornful ridicule. The firebrand and the attack on the mermaid would represent to the Freudian school the outpouring of sexual frustration. In the Jungian school it might represent a hidden memory of breaking something beautiful. Again, depending on the school of thought, the drowning could represent a return to the womb — or a realistic impression of what will happen if he lets his mind get so preoccupied with sex that he doesn't pay attention to his sailing skills.

As the dream repeats, we see the mind trying various solutions: a) Getting a life jacket into the boat; this helps with his preparedness and now he can sail with greater confidence when the fishing vessel goes by. b) Getting a fiancee. Now the phallic significance of the firebrand is revealed, for now it becomes the erect phallus and he does not need to hide his sexual frustrations under a euphemism, for she understands them.

The mind may try literally thousands of different combinations of the same dream before it is satisfied with it. These successive changes or successive approximations enable the dreamer to try various courses of action in the dream without actually having to go through the physical experiences. There are thousands upon thousands of different variations in repetitive dreams. Sometimes it will be yelling at the boss, after cringing for years; and the boss will be leading him away into a bright future. Sometimes the dreamer will be driving down the road, get distracted, and have an accident. The dream shows him the terror of the accident, the bigger-than-life blood and gore, without his actually having to experience it. The dream is a warning to the sailor, and it also shows him ways in which he can avoid disaster. He may be far too egotistical to do these things on a conscious level, but the CC is working. He is getting the message.

Symbolic: Our example dream is full of symbolism. If the dreamer is not a sailor, nakedness may represent an inability to face the truth. He may have high ideals that he cannot reconcile with the rather mundane job and lifestyle in which he finds himself. The boat adrift on the sea shows he must take a firm hold and get some strong direction into his life. The firebrand would remain a sexual symbol, but the assault on the mermaid could be read in several different ways: as an urge to show power over the "weaker" females in his life, or it could be that he has urges and emotions within himself that are soft and (to him) identified as feminine and "sissy." He has been told he must overcome these weaknesses to maintain his position as a macho man.

Interpretations of the symbolism of drowning sometimes symbolize a need to explore inner motivations, or it may be that in early life he lacked sufficient contact with his mother; but drowning in your own problems and the water representing tears and sorrow is also a valid interpretation.

The dreamer dreams his dream, and the symbolism in it is his own symbolism. It has meaning to him; but many times the dreamer cannot consciously admit the meaning of his dream, so by the time morning rolls around the dream messages are firmly suppressed. In suppressing them, unhappiness and even psychosis can result. The mind is pointing out problems that aren't going to go away. If they are suppressed, a mental or physical twitching will inevitably develop.

What Do Dreams Do?

By repetitive trial and error, dreams enable us to try various solutions to problems without having to go to the trouble of trying them in the physical world. They replace the actual experience with dream symbology and little playlets. Dreams also warn of the consequences of our actions or habits. If we realize in our subconscious minds that our sailing skills are weak, but we are too egotistical to admit it, dreams warn us what will happen as a result of our stubbornness.

Dreams identify root causes of problems. Consciously, "I do not want to admit I have weak feelings and sometimes I cry in sad movies," is replaced with the admission of these feelings. The dream shows the sailor that he must admit such feelings; otherwise he will drown.

Dreams reveal weaknesses. Only by repression can we hide from ourselves. If we are habitually careless in the way we sail our boat across the water, disaster will overtake us. The dream makes the result so much bigger than life that its warning can only be repressed or acknowledged; it cannot be ignored. Here the will to live is very important, and the subconscious fights for its own life by warning dreamers that we must make changes. When pushed to the limit, the dream symbology can become so violent that dreamers will forever give up the course of action that the dream warns about. The dream can turn dreamers in upon themselves. Dreams are a healthy way to solve problems.

If we pay careful attention to our dreams, we can see that they identify solutions to our problems and forecast the results of various actions we may take. If we learn to sail, and come to understand our inadmissible cross-gender characteristics, we will have a new love who will accept the erect phallus, and we will be able to brave the storm and float off together away from the wreck of the boat to a new and happier life.

The mind and its Consciousness Connection is a wonderful, extremely complex organism. Pay attention to its work; for it can save much misery and can direct us to a happier life.

Telepathic Dreams

Scientists the world over have studied the phenomenon of
people's dreams being influenced by others — the telepathic
dream. Using the students of our school as random subjects, over the years we have made nearly 10,000 attempts
at telepathically influencing other people's dreams. This is
a very large and random sample, and we had no control
over the selection of either the transmitting telepath or the
receiving dreamer. The experiment involved an attempt to
transmit the image of a bunch of red roses. In well over 75
percent of cases, in a dream during the night of the experiment the receiver actually saw a bunch of red roses. The
picture in which the roses were seen varied widely —
graveside bouquets, roses being trampled under foot, wedding bouquets, and diffuse romantic images of all kinds.
When we asked the participants on a second try to include
not only roses but also romance in the results they
reported, a startling 95 percent of those involved reported
success. The success rate was so high that it was not possible to gain any knowledge of the effect of distance between
the participants or such things as gender and age variations. At some future time we may continue the experiments. Until they are formally resumed, we would like you
to report any telepathic dream successes you have and the
circumstances surrounding them.

It is clear from our work that the dreamer can be influenced telepathically; and, though we cannot prove it, we
suspect that the closer two people are together, both physically and emotionally, the more they will influence each
other's dreams. This comes to a peak, we feel, when two
bedmates have a mutual orgasm and fall asleep in each other's arms. It would seem here that shared problems and
differences are subliminally transmitted back and forth and
come to fruition in shared dream meanings. Research into
this possibility will have to wait until a far more open attitude is prevalent than is permitted under present day Christian research grants!

Basic Interpretations

Although Professor Jung has shown that many generalized symbols are common, it is not judicious to take his guidelines as absolutes, for the mind will subtly modify them and give them meanings that are significant to only one person. When you dream, the symbols you see are the ones your own mind creates. They are unique to your background and experience. We do not deny that there are many common symbols which are universally recognized. But in most people's dreams, the symbols are uniquely personal and cannot easily be interpreted by a third party unless that third party is able to explore with the dreamer the meaning of the symbols he or she saw.

Further, on an almost minute-to-minute basis, symbology changes. You are on the street; you see a bad accident involving a blue car. In your own mind, subtle changes now occur in your feelings about the color blue. From a quiet, cool color it becomes a color of death and destruction.

Look at Table 11 on pages 210–213. These are the generalized meanings of various dream symbols. For instance: if you dream repeatedly of rain and water, in most cases this reveals that you are weeping inside about something, so you should analyze your life conditions to identify the cause of the tears and use the techniques we will describe to overcome problems. Similarly, if you dream of a rabbit in a negative situation involving someone of the opposite gender, it is quite probable that you have an unhealthy attitude toward making love. Acknowledging that this poor attitude exists, you can take steps to remedy it and meantime make allowances for yourself so as to feel more serene.

Remember that the messages in Table 11 should be modified by your own feelings about dreams. The set of interpretations we have provided should be used only as a starting point. When you become interested in this subject, you will find many themes of interpretation. It is a good idea to collect interpretations to develop your knowledge of the many ways that you can view symbology.

Table 11. Common symbolic meaning of dreams.

Symbol	Meaning
Accident	Usually indicates that a real accident is about to occur.
Animals	Depends on your feelings about the animal. Typically, Bees — Don't get stung Hogs — Greed Cats — Mysterious woman; jealousy Doves — Future peace Elephant — Memory; gentle strength Oyster — Wealth to be discovered Peacock — Too much pride Dog — Faithfulness or danger Small bird — Spirit Rabbit — Timidity
Apple	Desire, both sexual and for knowledge.
Basement or Cellar	Low level of development; the unconscious mind.
Battle or Aggression	Usually internal conflict; watch to see who wins.
Birth, Death, Bridge, Doorway	All symbols of transition and change.
Broom	Cleaning up; clearing the paths ahead.
Car or Carriage	Your physical body.

Table 11. Common symbolic meaning of dreams (continued).

Symbol	Meaning
Cane, Crutch, Sticks	A need for support.
Climbing, Classroom Exams	Learning and gaining in the spiritual side of life.
Clock	Warning of need for action.
Clothing and Nakedness	Depends on attitude; ranges from honesty through fear and embarrassment to sexual symbolism.
Crying, Rain	Sad event you have not faced. Need to grieve.
Dagger	Traitor; sometimes to a woman, a dominant male.
Dancing	Making love.
Drinking Water and Eating Moderately	Love; fulfillment; self-indulgence.
Drowning	A wish to escape, problems of the mundane world.
Eye	Self-examination; pass through eye to new realizations.
Falling	Not living up to your own goals; falling in other people's estimation.
Fire	Either fired up or anger at being frustrated.
Flying	With aircraft – rising above it all; Without aircraft – astral travel.

Table 11. Common symbolic meaning of dreams (continued).

Symbol	Meaning
Glass	Seeing into the future, either clearly or through a murky or clouded pane.
Graduation	Initiation, time to move on to a higher level.
Heart Attack	Either precognition or a romance.
Highway or River	Your life path; look to the sides to see progress.
House, Hotel	Your life, each room being a different area for you to examine. Attic represents head, lower rooms the lower limbs, kitchen is the stomach.
Ice	Frigidity; loneliness.
Journey	Quest for missing piece of a puzzle in your life.
Jury	Guilty conscience.
Key	The answer to a difficult problem.
Lost	Losing contact with the spiritual side of your life.
Missing a Boat, Plane, Bus, etc.	You are missing out; life is getting away from you.
Mountains	Challenges ahead.
Numbers	Write them down; they are important.

Table 11. Common symbolic meaning of dreams (continued).

Symbol	Meaning
Paralysis	You are stuck and afraid or unable to move.
Passenger	You are letting it happen, being just carried along.
People, Parade or Crowd	The people usually depict the many roles you play in your own life.
Rehearsal	Preparing for an important event.
Ring	Completion; devotion and love.
Ruins	Plans will go astray; despair.
Sexual Intercourse	Reconciliation of internal conflict.
Skeleton	Hidden problems; death.
Sleeping	You're missing something you ought to have, or you're not aware of something going on.
Snakes	Need for sex; or gaining wisdom.
Teeth	Depends on their condition. If rotten, falsehood; if clean and strong, loving kindness.
Water	If calm, peace; if stormy, troubles. Otherwise, spirit.
Witch	Mystery and power; supernatural aid.

Interpreting Your Own Dreams

With all these varied meanings, you may ask whether you can ever expect to interpret your own dreams. The answer is: not only can you expect to — but you must! For ignoring your dreams, especially the troublesome ones, can lead to disaster. The subconscious absorbs many day-to-day impressions that the conscious mind either ignores or rejects. Is the lover about to drop you? You may go on long after the affair is really over, hoping that some flame can be rekindled. Yet your dreams may be forthrightly telling you that nothing you can do will help, and that other person you ignored would better repay attention. Dream interpretation is best carried out with the aid of someone who is a trusted confidant — not, by the way, a spouse, lover, or a close relative; but failing this, you can examine your own dreams. Then with the passage of weeks and months you can build up meanings for your own symbology. The dream dictionary that we recommend you use[2] if you wish to pursue this investigation categorizes meanings, both ancient and modern, and has a wider range of interpretations than most. With its aid you can certainly interpret your own dreams, at least enough to get a general feeling for the problems and solutions that are being presented to you through your CC.

Interpreting Dreams for Others

Like any other reading, this is a private matter. Only the reader and the subject should be present. The dearly beloved spouse or the enamored lover should be firmly shut out of any dream counseling session. The dream that is presented over the dinner table can be dealt with only very superficially. If you announce you are a dream analyst, you will be besieged by people who need help; and only through their conscious and unconscious trust in the confidentiality

---

[2] *The Complete Dream Book* by E. F. Allen (New York: Warner Books, 1967).

and security of your joint work can they be made comfortable enough to discuss the true meaning of their symbology. Oftentimes the mildest virginal types will have dreams that are embarrassing and shocking to their conscious sensibilities. They will dream of being raped, or of raping someone else; they will kill or be mired in feces; they will eat live animals; and do many unbelievably ugly and disgusting things. You must never show any alarm or other emotion at these revelations, for the least hint of revulsion or disapproval will turn them off—and obviously these are the people who most urgently need help in getting inner and outer selves back together into a balanced whole.

Predicting from Dreams

Many dreams in and of themselves give the reader the information needed to predict the outcome of a specific course of action. To be most effective, dream prediction requires a series of dreams that should concentrate on the changes that occur over time.

Often it helps to diagram out the problem and to give the conscious mind some appropriate conclusions to work with. You can very easily learn to program your mind and that of your subject to give the visions you need. No matter if the subject's awareness takes the form of pictures, sounds, smells, tastes, or hunches, if the problem is drawn as a series of little cartoon sketches, the subject's mind will be able to follow the alternate choices and pick the one that most closely approximates an ideal solution, or even give ideas that offer another solution altogether—one that had not been considered. Look at figure 37 on page 216. It shows the problem in the little picture at the bottom of the figure—in this case an empty wallet, a common enough dilemma these days. The problem is compounded in this hypothetical case by the fact that the rent is due on Friday. Step 1 is to sketch various actions that would bring money in to pay the rent. In the case at hand, they range from selling blood at the blood bank, pictured as a little bottle full of blood; to selling

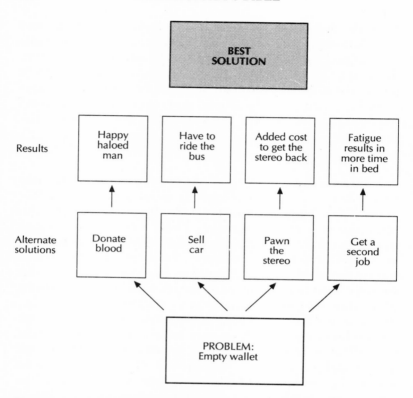

Figure 37.   Diagramming your questions.

the car, pictured as a car with a dollar-sign over it; to pawning the stereo, pictured as the stereo with three balls over it; to getting a second job, pictured as the weary stick figure.

Moving up the diagram, the next sketches show possible results of each action. Choice 1 shows a little fatigue and a happy stick-man walking away with a halo. Choice 2 shows the stick-man riding the bus. Choice 3 shows dollars going out to get the stereo back, with the dollar-sign drawn large to indicate that many dollars will be required. Choice 4 shows the stick-man in bed while others are out enjoying themselves. The box labeled Solution at the top of the diagram is to be completed in terms of the subject's visions.

Help the subject think up as many possible solutions and their consequences as possible. Think up wild solutions, extravagant solutions, barely plausible solutions — the more the better. Then have the subject review the sheet you have jointly constructed just before going to bed. During dreams or within twenty-four hours, an impression will suggest itself that specifically describes the solution to the problem.

· · ·

Dreams have been called the mirror of the Soul. They strip away many layers of learned social behavior and religious ethics. They can and do set the dreamer free to act out solutions in a logical manner. These solutions can range from outright bestial behavior to the highest level of selflessness. The more we repress things, the more we deny even to ourselves that some of our thoughts are contrary to attitudes we have been taught, the more we try to protect our egos by pretending that we are better than we know ourselves to be, the more dreams will tell us in the most vivid ways that we are kidding ourselves. Pride goes before a fall. If we can take the fall in a private dream, if we can acknowledge and understand it, then we can protect our egos by taking actions in the mundane world, approaching our problem from a new and different angle. If preservation of the better facade is important, it can be sustained. A result even more beneficial will be the end of self-delusion and a healthy feeling that we are making the most of the raw material at our disposal.

Chapter 12

The Prophet's Reality

Without a clear idea of the reality in which we all live, few if any conclusions can be reached as to whether you can succeed as a prophet. The first thing you should try to understand is time itself; for until you create your own hypothesis as to how time works, you can accomplish little. Intimately connected with time, the whole question of the space in which we live needs to be examined. For example, are we living in the only universe, or are there other universes on different planes which intersect ours?

Further, a hypothesis is needed as to *why* we are here; for only from this understanding can a system of ethics be established for the prophet and the subject.

Our working hypothesis may be suitable for direction in your own life. We are forever open to other hypotheses, however; today we like the one we have but we are in no way hidebound or fossilized. If you don't like ours, invent your own—and please tell us about it. At any rate, the following pages share some of our ideas about why we are here and why prophecy works.

The Sense of Time

Time is another one of those forgotten senses.[1] We all have such a sense; yet there is no organ with which we can associ-

---

[1] See page 1.

ate it, so it is very rarely investigated. Thousands of devices to measure time have been invented, perhaps because we do not experience time in the logical continuous passage of one second after another. When we are stimulated or fearful, time expands or slows down. The stimulation may be mundane (as when we impatiently watch the pot that never boils), or pretty emotional (as when death is threatened or an orgasm approaches).

We think of time as a continuum — the tape rolling from one reel onto another; the Future flowing past Now into the Past (not into Now, for Now has now gone). Yet the tape stops for us when we sleep, and apparently we can skip ahead and look at what is to come.

The expression "time line" is used for the time continuum in which we presently exist. We realize how variable this time line is when we realize that a future astronaut flying faster than the speed of light may in ten years of his life pass by 2,000 years lived by those who stayed behind on earth.

Some scholars propound the theory of an infinite number of parallel time lines existing in infinite universes around us. Every time chance takes a hand, they believe, a new time line is started. An example: if the sperm of that Roman soldier, Panther, had not fertilized the ovum of priestess Miriam, James would not have had a younger brother Jesus and a time-line universe without Christianity would be in parallel existence with ours. Attractive as that idea is, we cannot subscribe to it; for we cannot comprehend a system even as large as our multi-verse also containing an infinity of other multi-verses of which new ones are being created with every random pregnancy or murder.

Instead, we propose the theory that reality, the here-now, is created as we move along our time line by the thoughts of every being on that time line. The combination of thoughts that make up our reality is called the "consensus reality." Everyone believes that the earth is almost round and that it travels around the sun — therefore *ipso facto* it does. If everyone believed the earth was flat and that an entirely different set of physical laws applied, the earth would be flat. An illustration of this is the way people think of color. How do you know when I say, "The grass is green," that I see the same color you see? You may see a color that I would call red or blue, but you have been taught to call it green as I have been taught to call it green. The reality of green is therefore something we all agree is green, even though each of us perceives something different.

What evidence do we have to support our hypothesis? We believe we have the best, the most concrete proof available to date. It comes from an ongoing twenty-year experiment into the phenomenon of astral travel; in the experiment we have asked hundreds of subjects to report back on what they observed. The ongoing experiment includes the analysis of more than 6,000 trips by many different observers into the future. Our hypothesis on the time line is not just the idea of a few religious fanatics; but the scientifically evaluated and cross-correlated results of an ongoing experiment that has lasted many years.

Past, Present, and Future from Astral Travel

The mind can travel in time both forward and backward without restraint. The astral travel experiments show that this same "travel" can be duplicated by the spirit,[2] though spiritual travel seems to have some restrictions imposed on it. Scenes in the far past tend to fade into oblivion; scenes in the future, though bright and colorful, tend to be variable and changeable at the whim of the spirit's thought. Therefore it appears that what we call "here-now" is the crystallization of everyone's thoughts about what now is. As now disappears into the past and gets less attention paid to it, so it tends to fade away, but it does not cease to exist. Once the here-now reality construct has been made, it is like a permanent instant photo that slowly fades. There is evidence to

---

[2]The non-physical surviving ongoing part of every individual.

support the belief that the future coming along toward us on our time-line already has in it many pieces or constructs. By their future thoughts, for example, science fiction writers may fix such things as Dick Tracy's two-way radio or Jules Verne's rocket to the moon. As these predictions of the future come toward us, so the ideas become part of our here-now reality.

Let's see how our hypothesis works with some perhaps trivial examples. An expert predicts a shortage of toilet tissue. Housewives think, "There will be a shortage!" Instantly, a shortage exists.

A more subtle example deals with the favorite race-horse. Thousands of people think a particular horse will win a particular race; others believe another horse will win. In the actual event, victory goes to an outsider! How can this happen if the "consensus reality" is the law of the universe? Quite simple: the consensus reality of thought, or the total energy devoted to the favorite's winning, may be far less than the thoughts of the few people who worked like hell to get the outsider to the starting gate.

Yes, your thoughts affect the future—but so do the thoughts of every other living being. As the future becomes the present and fades into the past, so reality crystallizes. Your thoughts may be overpowered by millions of other thoughts put out by other living beings, or by the single very emotional thought of one person. The reality that you perceive is the combined effect of all those thoughts.

The inference is: it is not a matter of how many people are directing their energy into a particular idea, but rather how dynamic the thoughts are. The dynamic, go-getting business person or prophet sees his or her hopes and dreams come true, while the wishy-washy aspirations of most of us are foredoomed to being overwhelmed by the vague mental driftings we all indulge in.

A final example will point up what we may call the "media problem" with prediction. Weather trends seem to be leaning toward more rotten weather for longer spells than ever before. We believe this is the direct result of two influences:

1) The media constantly tell us what rotten weather we are having. Everyone thinks "rotten weather" — and it stays rotten.

2) Millions of people go to church and pray in winter for hot weather, and in summer for cold weather. No one should be surprised, then, that summers grow hotter and winters grow colder.

Using the consensus-reality hypothesis enables you to understand prediction, and to recognize the times when a prediction is likely to come true and when it is not. Only those predictions that have that extra umph, that extra dynamic feel about them, have sufficient strength to impact the consensus reality in the way that will make them come true. We are not talking now, of course, about predictions regarding the general day-to-day course of events; we are talking about those predictions that will make a significant impact in your own life or in the life of those around. From the methods we have offered you, you must pick the one that is most emotionally satisfying to you. Learn how to use it, not as a parrot, but in a dynamic, flamboyant, creative, satisfying way. When you do, the predictions will come true. When you read the cards, cast the *I Ching*, or look at smoke patterns and everything looks flat and dull, don't predict! Who cares about flat, dull predictions anyway? Since there is little or no emotion in them, they will have no impact.

A word of warning is appropriate here. Some people are negative-forecasters. That means that the opposite to what they predict will invariably happen. There is some psychological twist in their head that is difficult to explain, and in some people it is a near-permanent characteristic. Their forecasts are not necessarily negative in content; they are just opposite to what will happen.

Do not confuse these negative-prophets with doom-sayers who always claim that things are going to hell in a handbasket; these people should be avoided as you would avoid a plague, for they will truly make negative things happen around you. Consider Armageddon, which is surely the quintessential Christian doom-prediction. It has not happened yet, but because of it a handful of priests have frightened millions of people for hundreds of years. The effects, in terms of human happiness-levels, are worth thinking about.

Sculpting the Future

In examining various methods of prophecy, perhaps we have overlooked the obvious. Why not just let your mind travel to the future, see what is going to happen, and report it back? But this, too, in our opinion, is unethical; for we know from our extensive experiments that this actually does sculpt the future in these circumstances. You can go into your subject's future life and rearrange it in accordance with your prediction. It is true that as this future picture flows down the time line toward the present the consensus reality will make changes in it; but if you have firmly and dynamically implanted a future event in the consensus reality, a large portion of that event will come to pass.

Predictions should be made from the objective extrapolation of present mundane and psychic facts, sieved through your unconscious mind and brought forth by the Consciousness Connection to the subject through your chosen method of prediction. You must not act like a demigod and make people your puppets.

Why Are We Here?

Because we cannot figure out how this reality could have happened without some prime mover, we start with a belief in an Ultimate Deity. We may all be (as Hindu mysticism teaches) just the dream of a God, but even that god must have been formed by some God or Ultimate Deity.

The Ultimate Deity, the God beyond Gods, has no gender and is beyond our comprehension. It is so far removed from us that, as the ancient Magi said, "It is the

Thought you cannot think about." Because It is so far beyond our mundane level, It has no power to operate in the world. It is the Source from which we derive life, but It cannot make our lives any easier on this plane of reality.

We consider that a little piece of the Divine Fire which is part of the Ultimate Deity inhabits the body of each living thing. Although we can have no conception of what It is like, still our spirit strives to return to It. One way we can consider the Ultimate Deity is to think of It as the sum of all the spirit bits in all planes of existence. A development from this belief is that each tiny spirit bit grows by learning and is reincarnated to a higher level.

Progressive reincarnation forms a cornerstone of our personal belief. The concept is well summarized in a 12th century poem from the Mathnawi. An excerpt reads:

> I died as a mineral and became a plant;
> I died as a plant and rose to animal;
> I died as animal and I was a Man.
> Why should I fear? When was I less by dying?

Our research supports the Sufi belief expressed in the poem. The belief is also shared by all the major religions of the world — except contemporary Christianity.

The spirit — your spirit — is immortal. It never dies; it only grows. The spirit is separable from your body, as you know yourself. You tend to say, "I live," "I sleep," "I love," but you talk about "my arm," "my head," "my body." Patterns of everyday speech acknowledge that the spirit and the body are two separate entities. One of the most ancient holy books was first written in Sanskrit, and the Sanskrit itself was merely the writing-down of an oral tradition very much older. In that book, the Rig Veda, it is written that:

> A human being is like a driver in a chariot.
> The immortal soul is the driver;
> The chariot is the body;
> And the reins of the chariot are Wisdom.[3]

---

[3]Wendy O'Flaherty, *Rig Veda* (London: Penguin, 1982).

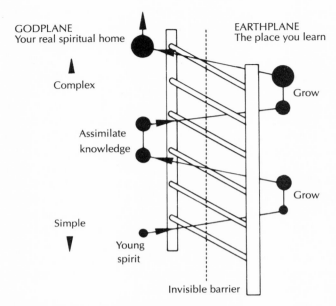

Figure 38.   Progressive reincarnation.

We believe that your destiny is determined by the way your spirit controls your body. Your spirit guides the actions of your body; the spirit is reincarnated on this earth plane in this specific body so it may learn what it is like to run a body around, what it is like to feel emotions such as pain, hunger, anger, love, and disappointment. When the body dies, the spirit casts it aside as a snake discards its outgrown skin; then very soon your spirit will take on another body to learn more lessons.

This idea may be described as the "boarding-school simile." Figure 38 shows it as a progression. The spirit comes from its home in Side where it has absorbed the lessons it learned in its previous earth-plane incarnation, and again inhabits a suitable body on the earth plane. When it has learned all it can from this body in turn, the body dies and the spirit returns to Side. Eventually, after many incarnations, the spirit is ready to progress to higher planes. Thus it is up to you to make sure that while the spirit is in a body, it undergoes as many experiences as you can arrange for it.

Looking at the over-all system, you see that the difference between a dead object and the most minute living thing, like a microbe, is spirit or "divine fire" which can be thought of as a piece of the Ultimate Deity. When the microbe dies, its spirit goes into Side. If the elemental spirit is judged ready to progress, it is given a more complex earth-plane identity to work with. So as the spirit learns, it is given gradually more and more complex living organisms to inhabit. At each level the spirit must gain complete control of the organism entrusted to it before it progresses. There is no backslipping from a complex to a simpler being; that is, if you are "bad," you won't transmigrate or reincarnate as a lower-level animal. Suicide (the refusal to attempt the tasks that are set and quitting instead) almost guarantees another whole reincarnation to complete the assignments required for graduation.

This upward growing learning process means that the Ultimate Deity Itself grows; for when the minute spark has completed all the growth it can get from all the entities on all the planet planes, it returns as a large flame of awareness to the All. Thus, as with all things in the natural way, growth through learning is the purpose — the very *raison d'etre* — of the universe and all its inhabitants.

This hypothesis leads to a different view of the place of human beings in the scheme of things. We are not above or below the rest of the beings in nature; instead we are part of a total scheme that involves a chain of progression. This gives most people a more comfortable feeling with their reason for being and a better understanding of why we should always remain in tune with other living entities. An additional benefit from this view is that, although we all still fear pain, we do not fear death — of ourselves, of a loved one, or of a project — for each death is an opportunity to start anew, to gain more wisdom by experiencing future tasks or life-times.

Knowing this underlying concept helps the reader guide his or her subject; for any time there is doubt, the reader should lean toward the path that will give the subject the most positive growth. Balancing between the growth available in several different paths is where the wisdom of the reader is called for. "Should I get married or go to college?" The reader must help each subject decide which path leads to the maximum spiritual learning, always remembering what Kahlil Gibran said in *The Prophet*: "Your pain is the breaking of the shell that encloses your understanding."

What Does the Future Hold?

If, indeed, this planet plane is designed as a classroom so little pieces of spiritual awareness can grow and learn in it, and if, indeed, this is a growth process, the future holds a far more complex world even than the world in which we presently live. The native on a desert isle lives a full and satisfying life — but has very few obstacles and difficulties to overcome. Moral decisions are simplified by a simple straightforward attitude about sex. Gradually his or her world changes. It becomes more and more complex, demanding ever more painful decisions. Because of the decision-making ability that most of us have developed in the world where we live today, we would find it comparatively easy to live on a desert isle. Although it might be satisfying, there would be a definite feeling of something missing. The spirit would languish. Admittedly we would enjoy the relaxation at first, but after a time we would start bringing elements of our civilization to the island. First we might build elaborate housing, then we might make up complex rules for social behavior and for the gathering and storing of food. None of these would be necessary, but they might satisfy an inner craving for growth and challenge.

How can you best equip yourself for the future? An easy way is to slow down your own life. Elect out of the blind mainstream rush and competition. Let others lead in the race of life, while you sit back and meditate on the effect the changes are having on moral and spiritual issues. This is a sound approach. If you want to lead in fighting the good fight, do it while you are young and resilient. As you grow older and wiser, withdraw from the forefront of the battle. Let others take over your position. Perhaps you should even move away from your power base. Whatever you do, don't let your spiritual growth stagnate. You should remain involved in the world, though not of it.

The Ethics of Prediction

People who seek a reading are generally in trouble and hoping for help, or at least looking for guidance regarding some decision. They should pay for the prediction in kind or in money — a sufficient amount so they will take notice. It is our strong feeling that no prediction should be done for less than the equivalent of $50. Occasionally you will want to break this rule, and of course you should follow your feelings. But following this guideline will immediately improve your results, because when the subjects pay, you both have an emotional involvement in the work. The old Witch who demanded her palm be crossed with silver (in a day when pennies, let alone silver, were rare) knew what she was about.

The wisdom in the reader's work manifests itself when you suggest a course of action that will lead to growth, happiness, and serenity for your subject. The distraught mother comes in with a dying child; the predictor sees clearly that the child will die. A blunt statement of the fact is not going to help the subject at all. Acceptance of death as graduation, acceptance of the organ bank idea, through which at least a part of her little one can live on, acceptance of the idea of increased freedom after the child dies, any or all of these alternatives will soften the blow and help the mother in the future. The reader is there to help, not just to thunder, "This is the word." By no means are we suggesting that you should always give a sweetness-and-light reading, for life certainly is not like that. Nor should you open a charity soup kitchen.

But you should advise and suggest, rather than simply saying, "Your idea for a new business stinks." When you see the
makings of a disastrous marriage, you can counsel delay or
suggest travel that will separate the ill-matched pair.

When you utter a very dogmatic prophecy and your
subject believes it, he or she has two choices: 1) to make sure
that it comes to pass by precisely following your ideas; or 2)
to make sure it does not come to pass by deliberately behaving in a contrary manner. Neither of these alternatives is
acceptable. They both stem from the dogmatic way the prediction was presented. Either way, you are the loser. You
should strive to encourage that the prediction is gradually
manifested as the present grows into the future — with the
subject's agreement.

How far should you go? That question can only be
decided by the situation between you and your subject. It is
important that you get the subject to follow you into the
prediction. All your faculties should be employed to make
sure the subject is "with" you. Watching his or her eyes,
especially the size of the pupils, is a help; pupils tend to
dilate when a path is reached that is acceptable, and tend to
contract when the path is not acceptable in his or her terms.
Body language will convey many other messages to you as
well.

Many readers feel too confident about impressions.
They become domineering: "You must do this. You will do
that." Such arbitrary dogmatic utterances are fit for a funda-
mentalist pulpit-pounder but not for a competent, compas-
sionate reader. No matter how strong your feeling is, no
matter how well equipped you feel to direct the life of
another, avoid such direction; for when you assume responsibility for the direction of his or her life, you are obliged to
continue the direction, thus becoming responsible for his or
her life and welfare. Moreover, any chance he or she may
have had to learn by doing and by making mistakes has been
eliminated. True, the subject will return for another reading, and another and another — and will now feel entitled to
reprimand you bitterly for every unpleasantness that befalls

him or her, and indeed to badmouth you all over town. There is a very fine line between gratitude and resentment. But it will be your own fault for taking over control of another's life.

If you find you have done this without being aware of it, you must break those controlling reins even if it means you give up the fees from a series of readings. Interference in a subject's life is altogether *verboten*. You must not take that attractive young man under your wing and make him your lover. The old psychologist's byword, "Would you feel so compelled to cure her sexual hangups if she were 90?" is very apt with respect to personal relationships between reader and subject. Such host-parasite relationships are all too easy to get into, but very difficult (and painful) to get out of. Unethical readers have raped and robbed their subjects, not only mundanely, but also mentally and spiritually. At all costs you must avoid such entanglements.

The underlying reason for existence, and for the underlying laws of the universe, can be summarized as growth through learning in a consensus reality. Lives follow natural courses. Personal problems that assail you today are not that different from those that troubled Stone Age humans. We didn't invent jealousy, desire, slyness, deceit, and conflict just last week. In a more complex society, both positive and negative emotions have to be dealt with and directed in a disciplined manner. Today people are troubled because of the state of the nation and its dearth of economic, moral, and spiritual resources. The competent reader fills an important niche in this time of turmoil, for you can help at least a few people regain stability and composure, and can direct them toward serenity through understanding.

As in school, suicide is equivalent to playing hookey; as in school, an assignment completed will not have to be repeated; after pain, you will recognize healing. If the reader makes a subject's life a little bit easier to comprehend, all is well; but if the reader completely smooths the path, the subject will learn nothing and his or her growth will cease.

Personal evaluation.

Attribute	Too Little	Just Right	Too Much	Reading
Self-reliance	Dependent	Autonomous	Brutal	_____
Honesty	Deceitful	Honest	Excessive	_____
Creativity	Passive	Creative	Destructive	_____
Appearance	Slovenly	Appropriate	Exquisite	_____
Personal relationships	Defensive	Warm	Intimate	_____
Group relationships	Shy	Effective	Aggressive	_____
IQ	Low	110	High	_____
Sincerity	Shallow	Sincere	Self-defeating	_____
Introspection	None	Occasional	Above others	_____
Temperament	Bovine	Stable	Volatile	_____
Initiative	Disciple complex	Suitable	Scattered	_____
Insight	None	Realistic	Unable to move	_____
Energy level	Limp	Achieving	Spastic	_____
Breadth of vision	Over-pessimistic	Realistic	Over-optimistic	_____
Dependability	Weak, unreliable	Dependable	Strong and reliable	_____
Initiative	Apathetic	Self-starting	No follow-through	_____
Attitude toward other gender	Hostile	Affectionate	Envious	_____
Sexuality	Indifferent	Healthy	Undisciplined lust	_____
Idealism	Expedient	Present	Quixotic	_____
Sense of proportion	Tangled in own underwear	Balanced	Overly analytical	_____
Money	Spendthrift	Sound	Miserly	_____
Domesticity	Traveler	Concerned	Over-dependent	_____
Loyalty	Friendless	Loyal	Parasite	_____
Courage	Coward	Courageous	Reckless	_____
Adaptability	Rigid	Flexible	Indecisive	_____
Sympathy	Cold	Sympathetic	Agape	_____
Forgiveness	Dogmatic authoritarianism	Appropriate	Over-tolerant	_____

Health evaluation.

Body Part	Left Side	Right Side	Body Part	Score
			Reproductive system	____
			Harmful behavior patterns	____
Foot			Urinary tract	____
Ankle			Digestive tract	____
Leg			Brain	____
Eye			Mouth	____
Nose			Teeth	____
Ear			Lymph system	____
Hand			Nutrition	____
Wrist			Rest	____
Arm			Exercise	____
Shoulder			Pelvis	____
Kidney			Back	____
Lung			Head	____
			Heart	____
			Liver	____
			Stomach	____
			Exposure to toxic substances	____
Overall			Physical	____
			Mental	____

Name:_____

Street:_____

City:_____State:_____

Phone:_____

Age:_____Gender:_____

Name: _____

Numbers: _____

Consonants: _____ Vowels: _____

Birth date: _____

1										
2										
3										
4										
5										
6										
7										
8										
9										
0										
11										
22										

Numericon chart is from *The Prophet's Bible* by Gavin and Yvonne Frost, published by Samuel Weiser, Inc.

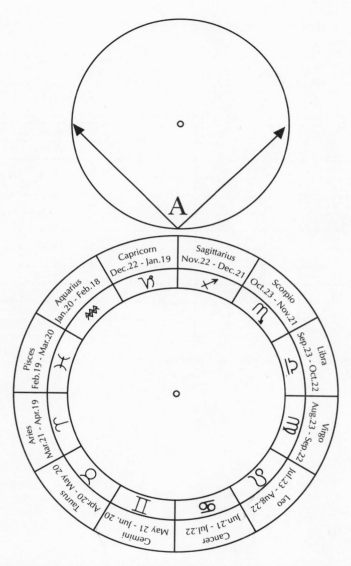

Your astromantic incompatibility dial. Cut out the dial at the top of the figure. Pin it to the center of the bottom figure. Place Point A on your birthdate. Arrows will indicate incompatibilities.

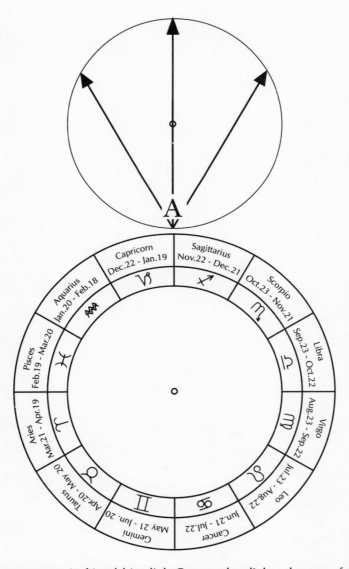

Your astromantic friendship dial. Cut out the dial at the top of the figure. Pin to the center of the bottom figure. Place Point A on your birthdate. Compatible friends and lovers will be found at the head of solid arrows.